T0132187

INDICTMENT OF THE U.S. FEDERAL GOVERNMENT

SENAN SHAIBANI

authorHOUSE®

AuthorHouse™
1663 Liberty Drive
Bloomington, IN 47403
www.authorhouse.com
Phone: 833-262-8899

Published by AuthorHouse 12/22/2023

ISBN: 979-8-8230-1672-8 (sc)
ISBN: 979-8-8230-1671-1 (e)

Library of Congress Control Number: 2023920620

Print information available on the last page.

A Foreword from the Family

Senan Shaibani was not just a promising scholar or a passionate activist to us—he was family. A loving son, caring brother, and a beacon of hope and inspiration to all who knew him. His determination to bring light to dark corners of the world was evident not just in his words, but in his actions.

This book is one of his greatest and cherished works. While he never saw his work completed, we decided that it would be in his honor to publish in its latest state to honor his lasting legacy.

While we grieve the immense void his untimely passing has left in our lives, we take solace in the fact that his voice and his message will continue to resonate through these pages.

It's our sincere wish that as you delve into this book, you come to understand the depth of Senan's convictions, the breadth of his knowledge, and the heart that beat for justice. May his words inspire others as much as his life inspired us.

-The Shaibani Family

Table of Contents

Table of Figures

Indictment of the United States federal government to preserve the world from the existential threat of greed, exploitation, and violence of the prime criminal power in the globe

American imperialism has opposed the most basic international laws, treaties, conventions, and declarations that protect the sovereign national rights of the Syrian Arab Republic and the Republic of Iraq to their human rights, territorial integrity, freedom from foreign invasions, breaches, and interference in the establishment and operations of their political and governmental systems. Representatives of the US regime need to face indictments for their crimes as the inheritors of the colonial legacy of genocide and slavery.1 A national and international tribunal must repudiate the federal government of the United States and the

---

[1] *This effort was inspired by the **International Tribunal for Indigenous People & Oppressed Nations in the U.S. 10/4/1992** Verdict: Found guilty by international jurists with US officials served indictments*

conspiracy for a New World Order founded on wars of oppression, bloodshed, genocide, colonialism, exploitation, major violations of fundamental rights, and the denial of the international legal right of self- determination to all sovereign and independent nations across the world. The US government has no right to exist as a legal and political entity for unprecedented war crimes, violations of international law, universally accepted principles, and most significantly Divine Law that supersedes the man-made law of white supremacists. This paper provides the legal basis to indict US officials pursuant to their own legal system and internationally accepted norms in a legitimate trial with the authority to implement the verdict. The United Nations has failed to enforce the UN Charter against the number one criminal organization in the world. Why has the UN passed resolutions in favor of the US and against oppressed nations that challenge named party? Why enforce legal standards against oppressed nations of the world but not the oppressor nations? The judicial decision of this effort will provide a foundation for future nations and peoples who seek redress against the US federal government for the commission of international crimes. ((38)(1)(d) ICJ) (Art. 92 UN Charter2).3

The Resistance of Syria and Iraq with their regional allies reserve the right to forcefully expel any American, NATO, or Zionist invasion that refuses to respect our right to self-determination that demands independence and the unconditional retreat of the US led occupation.

---

2   *United Nations, Charter of the United Nations, 24 October 1945, 1 UN XVI*

3   *Jihad Abdulmumit, How an international tribunal 70 years in the making found the U.S. guilty of genocide. Resistance Studies (2023)*

International standards of human rights law applied to domestic litigation will strengthen advocacy efforts for oppressed nationalities and raise consciousness about the necessity to overcome the limitations of the inherently unjust US legal system. Those who reside in the US settler state possess the power to organize for the establishment of a popular movement that will hold responsible the allegedly elected government that constitutes the primary enemy of humanity. The US police state has the highest rate of incarceration globally while it violently violates international law in the name of democracy. The corporate media that manufactures consent for illegal wars wants Americans to condemn the actions of states across the world yet ignore the unparalleled crimes of their own. Even though we possess more agency to challenge the government where we live than against any other thousands of miles away. US imperialism poses an existential threat as the principal contradiction to human liberation in the unipolar international system it seeks to impose. The struggle of Iraq & Syria represents the struggle for all of humanity for liberation from a global system led by the United States. Imperialism and neo-colonialism constitute the control of the world economy by monopoly corporations (headquartered in the US) whereby the capitalist class of the imperialist country violates international law with impunity against the sovereignty of nations and exploits their labor and steals their natural resources. No enforcement mechanism has manifested to effectively ensure the primary hegemonic power in the world respects international law but that will change as US power declines. The belligerent US regime donates the most to the United Nations which will obstruct efforts for the UN General Assembly to bypass their veto at the Security Council. But it was not the UN that ended the illegal invasion of Iraq or the unlawful occupation of Lebanon. It was revolutionary war that forced the invaders to leave in line with international law. The resistance forces of Iraq and Syria will hold highly ranked US officials accountable if we intensify our armed struggle and build effective specialized criminal tribunals. Solidarity efforts within America will facilitate this process that demands the dissolution of the US federal government for violations beyond comparison of the laws of all legitimate nations in blatant disregard of Native sovereignty it currently occupies. The facts that follow entail the legal grounds to hold the US federal government accountable even pursuant to their very own laws and internationally recognized entities such as the UN which has functioned as an accomplice to war crimes.

Table Of Authorities

Cases

Baker v. Carr, 369 U.S. 186, 278 (1962)

Advisory Opinion on Namibia (ICJ Reports 1971)

The Western Sahara case (ICJ Reports 1975)

Handschu v. Special Services

Reid v. Covert, 354 U.S. 1 (1956)

Filartiga v. Pena-Irala, 630 F. 2d 876 (2d Cir. 1980)

Rodriguez-Fernandez v. Wilkinson, 654 F.2d 1382 (1981)

Asakura v. Seattle, 256 U.S. 332, 341 (1924)

Sullivan v. Kidd, 254 U.S. 433 (1921)

Lauritzen v. Larsen, 345 U.S. 571 (1953)

Murray v. Schooner Charming Betsy, 6 U.S. 64 (1804)

The Paquete Habana, 175 U.S. 677, 20 S. Ct. 290, 44 L. Ed. 320 (1900)

The Republic of Nicaragua v. The United States of America

Statutes

Leahy law: 10 U.S.C. § 362

Leahy law: 22 U.S.C. § 2378d

International Emergency Powers Act

War Crimes Act of 1996 for Protecting Civilians

Telecommunications Act of 1996

Treatises

Protocol I of 1977 to the Geneva Conventions of 1949

1949 Geneva Conventions

General Assembly from November 1950 (resolution 377 (V))

Protocol 1 Article 4(A)(4) of the Third Geneva Convention

Resolution 3103 (XXVIII), 12 December 1973

1907 Hague Regulations (Protocol I)

Chemical Weapons Convention

Convention gainst Torture and Other Cruel, Inhumane or Degrading Treatment or Punishment

Convention on the Elimination of all Forms of Discrimination Against Women

Convention on the Rights of the Child

Declaration on the Principles of Int. Law Concerning Friendly Relations and Co-Operation Among States

Geneva Conventions Relative to the Treatment of Prisoners of War

Genocide Convention and the Geneva Conventions of 1949

Hague Convention for the Protection of Cultural Property in the Event of Armed Conflict of 5/14/1954

Hague Conventions of 1907

International Covenant on Civil and Political Rights

The Nuremberg Trials

United Nations Charter

United Nations Declaration of Human Rights

United States Convention on War Crimes and Crimes Against Humanity, Including Genocide

Universal Declaration of the Rights of People

Vienna Convention on the Law of Treaties

U.N. Resolution 2625 (XXV)

Constitutional Provisions

U.S. Constitution

US Practices Contrary to International Law

The United Nations (UN) Charter,[4] which deems colonialism a criminal act, represents the most significant international treaty the United States (US) has endorsed in theory. However, in the absence of an enforcement mechanism to ensure its full compliance, the UN fails as a medium for the oppressed to seek redress in regard to their grievances against colonialism.

For many years the US federal government has vetoed more United Nations Security Council resolutions and denied more resolutions from the General Assembly than any other member state in attempt to transform the United Nations into an organ of imperialism. Proposed

---

[4]   *United Nations, Charter of the United Nations, 24 October 1945, 1 UNTS XVI*

solutions to this problem suggest all sovereign nations effectively pass resolutions that restrict the right of the veto or alternatively to establish the Non-Aligned United Nations.[5]

The most fundamental international law within the current framework that exists in relation to the rights of a sovereign state entails the right to security in its territorial integrity or boundaries from foreign invasion. This right was identified in the UN Charter in article 2, section 4, and provides as follows:

All Members shall refrain in their international relations from the threat or use of force against the territorial integrity or political independence of any state, or in any other manner inconsistent with the Purposes of the United Nations.[6]

The United Nations Charter, as well as other treaties, principles, declarations, and international laws cited herein stand for the fundamental right of self-determination on

---

[5]   *We Want Our Freedom Anyway! On Political Prisoners, Human Rights, Genocide, the Crime Bill & Control Units. Dr. Mutulu Shakur (1997)*

[6]   *U.N. Charter art. 2, para. 4.*

behalf of all sovereign nations. Foreign state interference, which adversely affects the exercise of this fundamental right of self-determination, violates article 33[7] and article 2, section 4[8] of the UN Charter,[9] among other universally accepted norms.

Article 2, section 4, of the UN Charter has no ambiguity. The provision prohibits threats or use of force against either the territorial integrity of national sovereign geographic boundaries or sovereign political independence and self-determination.[10] The breach of territorial integrity often appears only as an overt military act, but other means such as proxy warfare and espionage breach the territorial boundaries in covert ways.

Similarly, while unilateral US-led sanctions against Syria and Iraq always appear as extraterritorial in their

---

[7] *U.N. Charter art. 33.*

[8] *See id. (speaking to refraining from threat or use of force against another sovereign nation).*

[9] *See id.*

[10] *U.N. Charter art. 33. ("All Members shall refrain in their international relations from the threat or use of force against the territorial integrity or political independence of any state, or in any other manner inconsistent with the Purposes of the United Nations.").*

enactment, they specifically seek to undercut and disrupt the internal domestic political power of the then-current government to adversely affect the sovereign political independence. The US settler state historically has parasitically depended on the lands and political economic systems of other nations.

All sovereign nation-states possess the right to exercise self-determination and security in their political independence of any foreign actor or nation-state under international law. *The Declaration of the Principles of International Law Concerning Friendly Relations* and *Cooperation Among States in Accordance with the Charter of the United Nations* (U.N. Resolution 2625) provides that "the principle of equal rights and self-determination of peoples constitutes a significant contribution to contemporary law."[11]

The UN constitutes an organization of nation-states, not a forum for the resolution of private or individual

---

[11] *Declaration of the Principles of International Law Concerning Friendly Relations and Cooperation Among States in Accordance with the Charter of the United Nations, G.A. Res. 2708(XXV), U.N. GAOR, 25th Sess., Suppl. No. 28, U.N. Doc. A/RES/2708(XXV), at 122.*

grievances of violations of its articles. Each of the UN members, all 193, receive representation by ambassadors with the authority to act on behalf of the nation-state each represents.

Significantly, other international treaties, principles, declarations, and international laws support the right to self-determination. For example, *The Universal Declaration of the Rights of People* (the "Algiers Declaration") provides that all people, oppressed people, "have an equal right to liberty, the right to free themselves from any foreign interference and to choose their own government, [and] the right, if they are under subjugation, to fight for their liberation."[12]

---

[12]   *The Universal Declaration of the Rights of People, Declaration of the Government of the Democratic and Popular Republic of Algeria Concerning the Settlement of Claims by the Government of the United States of America and the Government of the Islamic Republic of Iran, JUS MUNDI (Jan. 19, 1981) https://jusmundi. com/en/document/treaty/en-declaration-of-the-government-of- the-democratic-and-popular-republic- of-algeria-concerning-the- settlement-of-claims-by-the-government-of-the-united-states-of- america-and-the-government-of- the-islamic-republic-of-iran- claims-settlement-declaration-1981-algiers-declaration-claims- settlement-1981-monday-19th- january-1981.*

The occupation of Iraq and Syria represents but one example of the continuous state of war the United States was founded upon in the quest for land and capitalist profit. What started with the genocide and forced labor of Africans in violation of Native sovereignty, occupation of Mexico, and Puerto Rico has expanded into the war on Iraq and Syria. The so called "war on terror" takes place inside and outside the illegal borders of America for the financial expansion of US capital. The war on Iraq and Syria includes a war on the American people who pay the price in resources and their rights.

The United States has repeatedly violated the various provisions of the UN, such as articles 33 and 48,[13] by both unauthorized breach of the territorial integrity of Syria and Iraq and by violent threats and attempts to interfere with the political independence of Syrian and Iraqi sovereignty.[14] If the US can invade Iraq and Syria,

---

[13] *U.N. Charter art. 48. Outlaws the use of force unless authorized by the Security Council*

[14] *U.N. Charter art. 33, para. 1 (declaring that parties to any dispute shall first "seek a solution by negotiation, enquiry, mediation, conciliation, arbitration, judicial settlement, resort to regional agencies or arrangements, or other peaceful means of their own choice.").*

then how can American officials condemn the Russian policy toward Ukraine? The territorial integrity of Syrian and Iraqi sovereign borders was violated directly by the US military, allied militaries, and/or indirectly by mercenary armies for economic and political control of the region rich with resources, labor, and markets in which to invest surplus at the expense of the original inhabitants of the land. The US regime never rushed to end the Syrian issue: the more killed in the opposition, the army and the people, means a weakened Syria erased from the regional equation.

The violations to Syrian and Iraqi political independence manifest not only through tens of thousands of American bombs but also by direct unilateral blockades and trade restrictions. No legal basis or UN endorsement exists for indiscriminate violence nor draconian measures that involve virtually every category of life for the Syrian and Iraqi people. The violations of fundamental human rights are as follows:

1. Blockade imposed on the Syrian Arab Republic as a so-called State Sponsor of Terrorism in 1979;[15]

2. US blocked or restricted the Syrian government (and targeted Syrian entities as well as individual Syrians' access to important financial markets since 2004 (in violation of the Vienna Convention);[16]

3. US blocked exports to Syria since 2004;[17]

4. US blocked air travel with Syria since 2004;[18]

5. US blocked or restricted the Syrian government (and targeted Syrian entities as well as individual

---

[15] *Fact Sheet on Syria, The White House: Office of the Press Secretary (Aug. 18, 2011), https://obamawhitehouse.archives.gov/the-press-office/2011/08/18/fact-sheet-syria("Syria has been designated a State Sponsor of Terrorism since December 1979.").*

[16] *3 C.F.R. § 13338 (2004). Prof. Dr. Alena Douhan, Preliminary findings of the visit to the Syrian Arab Republic by the Special Rapporteur on the negative impact of unilateral coercive measures on the enjoyment of human rights, UNITED NATIONS HUMAN RIGHTS OFFICE OF THE HIGH COMMISSIONER (Nov. 10, 2022), https://www.ohchr.org/en/node/104160.*

[17] *Id.*

[18] *Id.*

Syrians) access to important raw materials and industrial resources since 2011;[19]

6. The US allied European Union banned exports to Syria or arms, goods, and technology for the energy sector, which also banned imports of Syrian oil and precious metals, and prohibited business and financial exchange with the Syrian energy sector since 2011; [20]

7. In 2011 US allied Australia imposed an arms embargo and a ban on the export of equipment and technology for Syrian energy sector— i.e., electric power production and monitoring telecommunications since 2011;[21]

8. US allied Switzerland imposed a siege that generally copied the blockade imposed by the European Union since 2011;[22]

---

[19]   *3 C.F.R. § 13572 (2011).*

[20]   *Council Decision 2011/782/CFSP, 2011 O.J. (L 319/56) (EC).*

[21]   *Autonomous Sanctions Regulations 2011 (Austl.).*

[22]   *Reuters Staff, Switzerland Imposes Sanctions on Syria's Assad, REUTERS (May 24, 2011) https://www.reuters.com/article/swiss-syria-sanctions/switzerland-imposes-sanctions-on-syrias-assad-idUSLDE74N26V20110524*

9. After 2011, US allied Canada prohibited importation of Syrian goods, exchange in particular forms of technology, and the export of items from telecommunications items to luxury products. The United States passed executive order 12606 despite the fact that *restriction of information violates the Berman amendment;*[23]

10. US has blocked or restricted Syrian government (and targeted Syrian entities in violation of the *Vienna Conventions*) access to property or interests in property since 2011;[24]

11. US enhanced the siege through an executive order against Syrian and Iranian individuals, state security apparatuses, and information and communications technology and blocked importation of US goods into the Syrian Arab

---

[23] *Canada Expands Sanctions Against Syria: News Release, GOVERNMENT OF CANADA (Oct. 4, 2011) https://www.canada. ca/en/news/archive/2011/10/canada-expands-sanctions-against-syria.html.*

[24] *3 C.F.R. § 13572 (2011).*

Republic and Islamic Republic of Iran by any persons in the United States since 2012;[25]

12. In 2019 the US placed secondary restrictions against non-US persons anywhere in the world who provide financial, material, or technological support to the Syrian people, Syrian government, or engage in transactions with it or who supply goods or services to the Syrian military forces or the energy sector, in addition to the blockade of property transactions along with the imposition of travel bans all loosely interpreted under the Caesar Syria Civilian Protection Act.

The results of illegal blockades and military interventions of the US, its allies, and proxies inflicted serious and continuous human rights violations against Syria and Iraq and their significant regional allies. Men, women, children, the infirmed, the elderly, without regard to the most basic human principles that the UN was designed to protect and defend. Like many American laws, defects in executive orders often employ broad operative

---

[25] *3 C.F.R. 13608 (2012).*

language that too often results in defective executions and near-nonexistent post-event responsibility. They intend to intimidate and prevent any persons or entities from any kind of support to a nation that has endured an unprecedented disaster of the greatest complexity ever in history. Executive orders entail prohibitions of section **203(b)(2) of IEEPA (50** U.S.C. 1702(b)(2)) which states: "donations, by persons subject to the jurisdiction of the United **States, of articles, such as food, clothing, and medicine, intended to be used to relieve human suffering"** except for anyone designated by the US federal government. Under what standard of justice will the United States restrict donations such as **food, clothing, and medicine, intended to relieve suffering** so as not to impair the US presidential ability to handle so called national emergenciesww

This indefensible war effort against independent Arab states reflects more than broken policies and bipartisan executive fascism. It reflects a reaction to the crisis of an exploitive system. For the US federal government to wage illegal war internationally it requires that repression intensify domestically to control internal opposition. The "war on terror" violates the very own constitution of the US government, by electronic surveillance, informants, FBI-police plans to combine federal, local, county police forces to form the Joint Terrorist Task Force to infringe upon civil liberties. The FBI instructs government media to clear and hide the presence of the JTTF in all reports designed to criminalize and demonize anti-imperialist organizational efforts that formed a critical factor to end the war on Vietnam.[26] [27]The pretense of "anti- terrorism" seeks to make acceptable the violations of all standards of human rights in the United States and abroad.

US sanctions and military aggression constitute a deliberate effort for the physical destruction of independent societies to gain economic and political control of the region for cheap resources, labor, and markets. Denis

---

[26] *Poirot, Collin. "The Anatomy of a Federal Terrorism Prosecution: A Blueprint for Repression and Entrapment." Columbia Human Rights Law Review, 8 Dec. 2020, pp. 61–96.*

[27] *Media hides role of JTTF when they joined the SWAT, and militarized agencies raid of my family residence with robots, surrounded me with soldiers armed with machine guns pointed at me, coerced us into interrogations, threatened us not to speak of their failure to find charges against me upon my return from Iraq and that I cease political expression*

Halliday who was the UN Assistant Secretary-General in the 1990s explained about Iraq, "We are in the process of destroying an entire society. It is as simple and terrifying as that."[28] Halliday went on to state that the economic embargo was "deliberately, knowingly, killing thousands of Iraqis each month. That definition fits genocide".[29]

Article I of the General Assembly Resolution 260 (A) (II) of the United States Convention on War Crimes and Crimes Against Humanity, Including Genocide (December 9, 1948). The most catastrophic sanctions in the history of the UN contrary to the very charter it was established upon was imposed on the Republic of Iraq throughout the 1990s. This embargo that received condemnation by the ICJ and lead to the resignation of several UN officials in protest of the uninhabitable atmosphere forced upon the Iraqi people

---

[28] *Patrick Cockburn, UN aid chief resigns over Iraq Sanctions, INDEPENDENT (Sept. 30, 1998), https://www.independent.co.uk/news/un-aid-chief-resigns-over-iraq-sanctions-1175447.html*

[29] *Mark Siegal, Former UN Official Says Sanctions Against Iraq Amount to 'Genocide'", CORNELL CHRONICLE, (Sept. 30, 1999) https://news.cornell.edu/stories/1999/09/former-un-official-says-sanctions-against- iraq-amount-genocide.*

that was exasperated by tightened restrictions by the US and Britain. Sanctions after the 2003 ground invasion continue against segments of the Popular Mobilization Forces, Iraqi leaders, and an arms embargo against the Iraqi people.

US Senator Richard Black recently confessed that his government schemed to destroy Syria through a variety of means that include the theft of wheat, oil, and gas to starve the Syrian people so that they die amid severe material conditions.[30] He states that ten years prior to the protests in 2001, the Pentagon drafted plans to overthrow 7 countries in the region: Iraq, Syria, Lebanon, Libya, Somalia, Sudan, and ultimately Iran.[31] By 2006 the US embassy schemed in Damascus to destabilize the Syrian Arab Republic.[32] Most recently, Prof. Dr. Alena Douhan, a UN expert in the Human Rights Council reported that over half the Syrian population has reached food

---

[30] *Schiller Institute, The Truth about the Syrian Crisis, SENATOR RICHARD BLACK (Mar. 23, 2021),* https://www.youtube.com/watch?v=zRf_PmExPJM.

[31] *Id.*

[32] *Id.*

insecurity with water shortages because of unilateral sanctions enforced by the United States alongside NATO and their regional allies. These acts violate ***Protocol I of 1977 to the Geneva Conventions of 1949 33*** which states that "[t]he civilian population and individual civilians shall enjoy general protection against dangers arising from military operations." This encompasses protection from attacks that "expected to cause incidental loss of civilian life, injury to civilians, damage to civilian objects, or a combination thereof, which would be excessive in relation to the concrete and direct military advantage anticipated."[34] Over 90% of the Syrian population now lives below the poverty line, their right to education adversely effected, their access to electricity significantly reduced, the quality of the healthcare system devastated, with corruption and inefficiency of foreign humanitarian organizations that relate to oppressed people as helpless victims to profit from rather than organize as political agents empowered to effectively change their conditions. **The US should act on an emergency basis to permanently lift the sanctions**

---

[33]   *1124 U.N.T.S. 3.*

[34]   *1124 U.N.T.S. 3. at art. 51, 5.*

on Syria to save the innocent lives of millions in dire circumstances produced by an international alliance of US capital that still curtails shipments of materials into and outside of Syria despite all false impressions.

Protocol 1 Geneva Conventions 1977

Article 54: Protection of Objects Indispensable to the Survival of the Civilian Population

1. Starvation of civilians as a method of warfare is prohibited.

2. It is prohibited to attack, destroy, remove or render useless objects indispensable to the survival of the civilian population, such as foodstuffs, agricultural areas for the production of foodstuffs, crops, livestock, drinking water installations and supplies and irrigation works, for the specific purpose of denying them for their sustenance value to the civilian population or to the adverse Party, whatever the motive, whether in order to

starve out civilians, to cause them to move away, or for any other motive.[35]

The broad spectrum of sanctions imposed by Western imperialism developed for decades against the Syrian Arab Republic particularly and Resistance Axis generally after years of failure to end their support to regional resistance movements against imperialism and Zionism. The US has deliberately acted to produce domestic conditions conducive to infiltration and violent insurrections. The US axis imposes genocidal sanctions against oppressed nations as they recover from its catastrophic wars in Syria and Iraq yet criminalizes the constitutional right to peacefully boycott, divest, and sanction the illegal Israeli occupation[36]. US and Israeli settler colonialism both possess and use nuclear and chemical weapons unlike any other nation on earth yet face none of the consequences Iraq and Syria suffer from collectively for false allegations about weapons of mass destruction. The only nation to

---

[35] *Protocol 1 Geneva Conventions 1977. Article 54 (2): Protection of Objects Indispensable to the Survival of the Civilian Population*

[36] *Texas Anti-BDS Bill 85(R) HB 89. Anti-BDS legislation has passed in over 20 states*

obstruct the Biological Weapons Convention was the US yet just the idea of nuclear energy acquired by a major ally (Islamic Republic of Iran) to Iraq and Syria has incurred the illegal use of force and increased threats.[37]

Article 2

The Organization and its Members, in pursuit of the Purposes stated in Article 1, shall act in accordance with the following Principles.

1. The Organization is based on the principle of the sovereign equality of all its members....

2. All Members shall settle their international disputes by peaceful means in such a manner that international peace and security, and justice, are not endangered.

---

[37] *Fred Charatan, US rejects biological weapons convention protocol, NATIONAL LIBRARY OF MEDICINE, (June 2, 2001)* https:// www.ncbi.nlm.nih.gov/pmc/articles/PMC1173329/; *U.S. rejects biological weapons checks, REUTERS (Dec. 9, 2009)* https://www. reuters.com/article/us-arms-biological/u-s-rejects-biological-weapons-checks-idUSTRE5B82DG20091209.

3. All Members shall refrain in their international relations from the threat or use of force against the territorial integrity or political independence of any state, or in any other manner inconsistent with the Purposes of the United Nations.[38]

1. The Organization based on the principle of the **sovereign equality of all its members**.
The U.S. violated Principle 1 when it violated the territorial integrity of Syria through covert CIA support for foreign mercenaries in Operation Timber Sycamore and Pentagon support for Train and Equip Program which has international implications in acts of violence.[39]

2. All Members, to ensure to all of them the rights and benefits resulting from membership, shall fulfill in good faith the obligations assumed by them in accordance with the present Charter.
The U.S. violated Principle 2 when it violated the territorial integrity of Syria through support of foreign

---

[38] *U.N. Charter art. 2.*

[39] *Mehdi Hasan, Everyone Is Denouncing the Syrian Rebels Now Slaughtering Kurds. But Didn't the U.S. Once Support Some of Them?, INTERCEPT, (Oct. 26, 2019) https://theintercept.com/2019/10/26/syrian-rebels-turkey-kurds-accountability/.*

occupation of Syrian land by Israeli, British, French, Turkish, and NATO allies.[40]

3. All Members shall **settle their international disputes by peaceful means** in such a manner that **international peace and security, and justice, face no danger**.

The U.S. violated Principle 3 when it insisted on a military rather than political solution and violated the territorial integrity of Syria by military ground invasion and reconnaissance aircraft that occupied Syrian airspace and bombed the interior territories of Syria with internationally outlawed chemical weapons.[41]

Article 33

1. The parties to any dispute, the continuance of which is likely to endanger the maintenance of international peace and security, shall, first of all,

---

[40] *United States Strategy and Military Operations to Counter the Islamic State in Iraq and the Levant and United States Policy toward Iraq and Syria: Before the Comm. on Armed Services, 114th Cong. (2015).*

[41] *Jon Mitchell, Poisoning the Pacific: The US Military's Secret Dumping of Plutonium, Chemical Weapons, and Agent Orange (2020).*

seek a solution by negotiation, enquiry, mediation, conciliation, arbitration, judicial settlement, resort to regional agencies or arrangements, or other peaceful means of their own choice.

2. The Security Council shall, when it deems necessary, call upon the parties to settle their disputes by such means.[42]

4. All Members shall refrain in their international relations from the threat or use of force against the territorial integrity **or** political independence **of any state**, or in any other manner inconsistent with the Purposes of the United Nations.
And the U.S. violated Principle 4 when it violated the territorial integrity of Syria through the military occupation of northeastern Syria where it now openly loots vast amounts of Syrian oil and resources while it seeks to partition Syria.[43]

---

[42] *U.N. Charter art. 33.*

[43] *The Cradle: Routes of US tankers stealing Syrian oil unveiled, AL MAYADEEN ENGLISH (Nov. 15, 2022), https://english.almayadeen.net/news/politics/the-cradle:-routes-of-us-tankers-stealing-syrian-oil-unveile.*

With regards to resolution 2401 that demands a political solution to end the humanitarian catastrophe[44] and pursuant to the Article 51 of the UN Charter: nothing in the Charter shall obstruct the right of self-defense if an attack occurs against a Member of the United Nations, until the Security Council has attempted to enforce international peace.[45] This refusal of a political resolution means the continuation of the armed conflict and more destruction and death for Syria and an international crisis of migration.

Syria and Iraq share the right to self-defense with all legal means.[46] An illegitimate colonial and military occupation led by the U.S. continues to violate the territorial integrity of the Syrian and Iraqi Republics which possess the right to respond. Both share the right to defend the territories by different means such as judicial

---

[44]   *S.C. Res. 2401 (2018).*

[45]   *U.N. Charter art. 51 ("Nothing in the present Charter shall impair the inherent right of self-defence if an armed attack occurs, until the Security Council has taken measures necessary to maintain international peace and security.").*

[46]   *8188th Security Council Meeting. 24 February 2018 in reference to resolution 2401 (2018)*

action, direct political action in the mass form of boycotts, strikes, marches, solidarity campus sit-ins, blockades of government facilities, disruption of US weapons production, armed struggle in the persistent attacks against U.S. military bases, and destruction or blockade of convoys pursuant to Article 51 of the Charter.[47] [48]

The Syrian Government took all de-escalation efforts pursuant to twenty-nine other Council resolutions — that includes thirteen on counter-extremism — that require implementation to protect the lives of Syrians and an end to the violence.[49] All states need to sever ties with their separatist factions and the Israeli occupation of Syria to respect the territorial integrity of the nations that raised Europe out of the Middle Ages. On what legitimate basis can they claim to protect their borders from migrants displaced by their destructive intervention so long as they send occupation troops and foreign fighters who

---

[47] *U.N. Charter art. 51*

[48] ***US military convoys forced to retreat after Syrian troops block** road in Hasakah, 2022 WLNR 37345437*

[49] *Resolution 2178 (2014) Adopted by the Security Council at its 7272nd meeting, on 24 September 2014*

trespass into Syria and commit war crimes? The Syrian Arab Army retains the right to respond to attacks by such mercenaries which some Council members most notably the US supported and even practiced the state terrorism they claim to oppose only by lip service and never by any actions.

The violations perpetrated by foreign mercenaries, roughly 360,000 who invaded the country and in the name of "protests for democracy" with US support, posed a serious threat to the lives of 8 million people in Damascus alone.[50] The Syrian government has the responsibility as a State towards Syrian and Palestinian citizens to defend their homeland. Syria exercised the legitimate right, took measures to protect civilians, allowed their safe exit through humanitarian corridors unlike the US campaign against Raqqa where white phosphorus was

---

[50] *Shaheen, J. M. (2016, October 22). More than 360,000 foreign fighters have fought the Syrian Army" Firil Center for Studies FCFS, Berlin, Germany: Firil Center For Studies FCFS Berlin Germany: Retrieved November 14, 2022, from https://firil.de/360-000-foreign-fighters-fought-syrian-army-firil-center-studies-fcfs-berlin-germany/*

deployed indiscriminately.[51] The regimes of the US, the UK, and France must cease strategic plans aimed at the invasion and partition of the Syrian nation after they failed to divide Iraq[52]. The Iraqi & Syrian struggle for independence and liberation belongs to the revolution of the oppressed and exploited masses of the greater Arab nation against oligarchies, capitalism, and imperialism.

Military aggression by anyone against Iraq or Syria violates the Article 39 of chapter 7 of the UN Charter which states that the Security Council constitutes the only body entrusted and mandated with the very noble mission of peace, security, and prevention of aggression.[53] The UN Charter designates only the Security Council to exclusively possess the authority to deal with threats

---

[51] *Iraq/Syria: Danger From US White Phosphorus: Take All Needed Measures to Minimize Civilian Harm, HUMAN RIGHTS WATCH (June 14, 2017), https://www.hrw.org/news/2017/06/14/iraq/syria-danger-us-white-phosphorus.*

[52] *Houston National Public Library (2006, September 29).* **Sen. Biden: Divide Iraq into Three Regions***. NPR. Retrieved December 22, 2022, from https://www.npr.org/2006/09/29/6166796/sen-biden-divide-iraq-into-three-regions*

[53] *U.N. Charter art. 39 "The Security Council shall determine the existence of any threat to the peace, breach of the peace".*

to the peace, breach of the peace or act of aggression. Not the United States or any other client state to aggress upon any nation member of the United Nations on baseless allegations. Biden, like Trump, Obama, and Bush before him continue to undertake military activities in Syria and Iraq, a gross violation of the Security Council Resolution 2118.[54] Democrats and republicans both serve as administrators of the same colonial system only with different strategies to preserve the United States federal government that implements jurisdiction illegally.

The Republic of Nicaragua v. The United States of America demonstrated to the International Court of Justice that the U.S. regime financed violent operations against Nicaragua through the contras that waged war at the behest of Washington D.C. in the 1980s.[55] The ICJ found that America violated customary international law for interference within Nicaragua through the unjustifiable use of force that breached the sovereign rights of the indigenous nation through both overt and

---

[54] *S.C. Res. 2118 (Sept. 27, 2013).*

[55] *Military and Paramilitary Activities in and Against Nicaragua (Nicar. V. U.S.), Judgement, 1986 I.C.J. Rep. 14, (June 27).*

covert operations.[56] The ICJ ruled the United States owed the Republic of Nicaragua reparations. The ICJ dismissed the excuse of self-defense fabricated by the US in attempt to justify the morally reprehensible violence. The US involvement in covert operations in Iraq and Syria through programs such as Operation Timber Sycamore or Train & Equip replicates the same international law breaches against human dignity under *Nicaragua v. US*.[57] The CIA ran classified Timber Sycamore weapons supply operations.[58] The program was established prior to the intervention of allies formally invited by the Syrian government to defend the country against sectarian death squads that unlawfully entered the country to commit major crimes under the supervision of the US.[59] The Special Activities Division of the CIA ran the program,

---

[56] *Id.*

[57] *Comm. of U.S. Citizens in Nicaragua v. Reagan, 859 F.2d 929 (D.C. Cir. 1988)*

[58] *Mark Mazzetti, Adam Goldman & Michael S. Schmidt, Behind the Sudden Death of a $1 Billion Secret C.I.A. War in Syria, N.Y. TIMES, (Aug. 2, 2017) https://www.nytimes.com/2017/08/02/world/middleeast/cia-syria-rebel-arm-train-trump.html.*

[59] *Id.*

which trained thousands of mercenaries, according to US sources.[60] In 2013, The president gave the CIA a covert order to undermine the Syrian Arab Republic just as administrations before him attempted decades prior.[61] The Pentagon further trained "moderate rebels" to fight ISIS via the Train and Equip Program. Under these facts, the US, again, has breached customary international law and the Articles 2(4) and 33 of the UN Charter of the United Nations for armed interference in the affairs internal to a sovereign country by support to foreign mercenaries who invaded Syria and committed acts of genocide.[62] The Leahy laws prohibit governmental support towards any foreign armed forces if proof exists that such units

---

[60] *Mark Mazzetti, Adam Goldman & Michael S. Schmidt, Behind the Sudden Death of a $1 Billion Secret C.I.A. War in Syria, N.Y. TIMES, (Aug. 2, 2017) https://www.nytimes.com/2017/08/02/world/middleeast/cia-syria-rebel-arm-train-trump.html.*

[61] *Stephen R. Weissman, Covert Action, Congressional Inaction: The Intelligence Committees Shouls Do Their Jobs, FOREIGN AFFAIRS, (Dec. 2, 2020) https://www.foreignaffairs.com/united-states/covert-action-congressional-inaction*

[62] *Patrick Higgins, The War on Syria, JACOBIN (Aug. 27, 2015) https://jacobin.com/2015/08/syria-civil-war-nato-military- intervention.*

violated human rights with impunity.[63] Well documented crimes against humanity of the so called "moderate rebels" sponsored by US imperialism constitutes a violation of the Leahy amendments.[64] The US regime illegally assisted and subcontracted the war on Syria to Turkish, British, French, NATO and Zionist forces who continue to violate human rights as they violate the territorial integrity of Syria.[65] US marine forces that occupied Nicaragua engaged in torture similarly to the reprehensible abuse of the Iraqi men, women, girls, and boys at Abu Ghraib and elsewhere in shameless disregard for the very abuses that US officials claimed to liberate Iraq from.[66]

Reports emerged of Syrian children kidnapped, abused, and shot to death in northeastern Syria by the US occupation in violation of the most basic human standards with the Syrian Democratic Forces where the oil wealth

---

[63] *22 U.S.C. § 2378; 10 U.S.C. § 362.*

[64] *Id.*

[65] *Ali Kadri: Imperialism with Reference to Syria (2019).*

[66] *Richard Grossman. "Nicaragua: A Tortured Nation" Torture, American Style. Publication #3 Historians Against the War*

mostly exists.[67] The SDF commits abuses unreported in Western media that glorifies and whitewashes their crimes to garner appeal for a partitioned and dismantled Syria.[68] Arab youth I spoke to in Damascus testify that they endured and witnessed physical abuse by these separatist militias that denied them water and food which demonstrates yet another breach of US law defined by the Leahy amendments.[69] [70] These militias marketed through Western media represent only one end of the Kurdish political spectrum that serves US commercial interests. The sanctioned Syrian General Intelligence Directorate supported the Kurdistan Workers Party (PKK) against

---

[67] *Amnesty International, "Syria: Armed Group Recruiting Children in Camps "August 3, 2018 https://www.hrw.org/news/2018/08/03/syria-armed-group-recruiting-children-camps (January 4, 2023)*

[68] *2022, June 9 "SDF murders school student in Deir Ezzor, Syria" Al-Mayadeen English. https://english.almayadeen.net/news/politics/sdf-murders-school-student-in-deir-ezzor-syria*

[69] *2022, December 26 "Syrians Urge Immediate Expulsion of US Occupation Troops" Al-Mayadeen English. https://english.almayadeen.net/news/politics/syrians-urge-immediate-expulsion-of-us-occupation-troops*

[70] *Interview with traumatized Syrians displaced from Qamishli whom the Syrian Arab Army provided refuge from the abuse of US backed militias*

the unrepresentative government of Turkey then again most recently in the battle for Afrin.[71] The US regime condemns the PKK as a terrorist organization where most Kurds reside in Turkey because the major NATO base it provides imperialism but not in Syria, Iran, or Iraq whose armed forces oppose colonial designs.

Western intelligence and the Mossad support offshoots of the PKK against Syria and Iraq to undermine the Resistance Axis in the very name of national liberation denied to Native Americans.[72] The Israeli occupation and the Erdogan regime exchange weapons in an agreement to combat Kurdish and Palestinian so called "terrorists" respectively to serve the envisioned U.S. colonial order that the Resistance Axis has disrupted.[73] Factions that belong to the Popular Mobilization Forces consistently strike

---

[71] *Mehmet Orhan (2014) Transborder violence: the PKK in Turkey, Syria and Iraq, Dynamics of Asymmetric Conflict, 7:1, 30-48, DOI: 10.1080/17467586.2014.909946*

[72] *Matar, Linda & Kadri, Ali. (2019). Syria: From National Independence to Proxy War. 10.1007/978-3-319-98458-2.*

[73] *Eisenstadt, M. (1993). Turkish-Israeli Military Cooperation: An Assessment. The Washington Institute for Near East Policy, Policy Analysis (Policy Watch 262), 3. https://doi.org/Policy #262*

NATO led Turkish bases in solidarity with the PKK.[74] I spoke with Iraqi Kurdish and Arab Sunni fighters in the Popular Mobilization Forces at the Sayyedah Zainab (AS) Shrine whose very existence refutes the reductionist Western media narrative which acts as an associate in major war crimes.[75]

In my interview with the Kurdish leader of the Syrian Communist Party in Damascus, he stressed the duty of the Syrian Kurdish people to aid the struggle of the Syrian Arab Republic against imperialism. He questioned how governments engage in dialogue with the illegal Zionist entity while deny any peaceful political solution or negotiations with the legitimate Syrian government.[76]

---

[74] *Resistance Axis Brigades "The Free of Sinjar" in Solidarity with the PKK from the Iraqi Resistance factions that opposed the US invasion and ISIS who now strike Turkish NATO bases*

[75] *Firsthand Account of Shi'ite Kurdish and Arab Sunni members of the Popular Mobilization Forces who testified US forces struck their locations as the air force of ISIS*

[76] *Kurdish Leader of the Syrian Communist Party based in Damascus, founded by the Syrian Kurdish Khaled Bekdash, advocated a united front against imperialism in defense of the Syrian state and for the central government to ultimately make concessions to the Kurdish people in their cultural rights through education of their language and ID cards*

Engineered sympathy from segments of the western left for the YPG in Rojava that suddenly appeared in 2014 complimented the invasion of northeastern Syria by US forces as another major infringement of the territorial integrity of the Syrian state. This not only hurt the Kurdish cause but committed genocide against Arab majority in Raqqa where the US military openly used chemical weapons. [77] American claims to support Kurdish national liberation, as if Arabs designed Sykes Picot, only amounts to support for American protectorates that balkanize revolutionary nations.

The Article 20 of the International Covenant on Civil and Political Rights requires that any advocacy of national, racial or religious hatred that constitutes incitement to discrimination, hostility or violence shall be prohibited by law.

American intelligentsia promotes support for the construction of US military bases on Syrian soil and

---

[77] *Human Rights Watch.Iraq/Syria: Danger from US White Phosphorus. © 2017 by Human Rights Watch.*

the ethnic cleansing of Arabs[78] in the name of Kurdish liberation instead of support for the right to self-determination and national liberation of the internal colonies that seek the secession from the US federal government. Through the reunification of Mexico, the establishment of New Afrika, Puerto Rican, Hawai'ian independence, and the sovereignty of Native Nations.[79] [80]

The UN Charter amounts to the highest incumbent treaty in international law. The US has ratified the UN Charter on August 8th, 1945. Upon ratification, the UN Charter and the written content developed as the Supreme Law of the Land in the US under Article II, clause 2 of the US Constitution with the force and effect of federal law.[81] ***The Charming Betsy*** demonstrated this when the US Supreme Court declared that an act of Congress

---

[78] *Korybko, A. (2017). US Backed YPG Kurds are ethnically cleansing Arabs from Raqqa, and the world is silent. Global Research, June 15, 2017.*

[79] *Verdict of the International Tribunal of Indigenous Peoples and Oppressed Nations in the USA.*

[80] *Verdict of the Special International Tribunal on the Violation of Human Rights of Political Prisoners and Prisoners of Wars in United States Prisons and Jails.*

[81] *U.S. Const. art. II, cl. 2.*

should never violate a treaty signed by the US if any other possible construction exists. However, the United States still refuses to ratify basic international declarations that protect the human rights it uses as a pretext for military occupations. The US federal government has failed to ratify the **International Convention on the Suppression and Punishment of the Crime of Apartheid (1973)**[82], the **International Covenant on Economic, Social, and Cultural Rights (1966)**[83], the **Convention on the Elimination of All Forms of Discrimination Against Women (1979)**[84], **Convention on the Reduction of**

---

[82] *UN General Assembly, Status of the International Convention on the Suppression and Punishment of the Crime of Apartheid., 13 December 1976, A/RES/31/80, available at: https://www.refworld. org/docid/3b00f0382c.html [accessed 5 January 2023]*

[83] *UN General Assembly: (1966). International Covenant on Economic, Social, and Cultural Rights. Treaty Series, 999, 171.*

[84] *Citation: UN General Assembly, Convention on the Elimination of All Forms of Discrimination Against Women, 18 December 1979, United Nations, Treaty Series, vol. 1249, p. 13, http://www.un.org/ womenwatch/daw/cedaw/cedaw.htm.*

Statelessness (1961)[85], refused to sign onto the universally accepted **Genocide Convention**[86] for forty years, and has yet to ratify the American Convention on Human Rights[87]. The US discontinued all participation in the 2015 Paris to mitigate climate change even though the US constitutes the primary polluter on earth through the mass waste of the US military. The US needs to face an indictment and subsequent restoration of Native Sovereignty for grave crimes against humanity as the

---

[85] *UN High Commissioner for Refugees (UNHCR), Preventing and Reducing Statelessness: The 1961 Convention on the Reduction of Statelessness, March 2014, available at: https://www.refworld.org/docid/4cad866e2.html [accessed 5 January 2023]*

[86] *United States. Congress. Senate. Committee on Foreign Relations. The Genocide Convention : Hearing before the Committee on Foreign Relations, United States Senate, Ninety-Seventh Congress, First Session on Ex. O, 81-1, the Convention on the Prevention and Punishment of the Crime of Genocide, Adopted Unanimously by the General Assembly of the United Nations in Paris on December 9, 1948, and Signed on Behalf of the United States on December 11, 1948. Washington :U.S. G.P.O., 1982.*

[87] *Organization of American States (OAS), American Convention on Human Rights, "Pact of San Jose", Costa Rica, 22 November 1969, available at: https://www.refworld.org/docid/3ae6b36510.html [accessed 5 January 2023]*

number one enemy of all humankind that preaches the "human rights" it refuses to ratify.

The US regime breached the UN Charter Article 2(4)[88] notwithstanding justifications grounded in self-defense under Article 51[89], Chapter VII of the UN Charter, and humanitarian intervention.

Millions of people in America suffer from poverty, unemployment, lack of access to education, health care, and social benefits while trillions of US dollars fund violent violations of international law and US law. US police train with Israeli occupation forces guilty of war crimes in violation of the Leahy laws and then return to supposedly "enforce the law" as they incarcerate and violate the rights of the poor for petty non-violent crimes.[90] US law enforcement represses peaceful political dissidence and curtails the "freedom & democracy" that Iraq was illegally transgressed upon to supposedly protect. If someone shoots an officer or occupation soldier in their oppressed community then the state will railroad them

---

[88]   *U.N. Charter art. II, 4*

[89]   *U.N. Charter art. 51*

[90]   *22 U.S.C. § 2378d; 10 U.S.C. § 362.*

off to slavery in concentration camps until death if not immediately kill them. But if airmen bomb thousands of Iraqis and Syrians with chemical weapons, then the state rewards them honorary titles. When a poor man holds up a bank to expropriate wealth stolen from his economic class, he faces life in state prison but when a banker embezzles thousands, he will spend a fraction of that time in a more comfortable jailhouse.[91] Why build the most private prisons in the world at a far higher rate than universities that cost more in America than in any other country? Why cut federal funds to universities if they lack recruitment to a military industrial complex that commits genocide against entire nations?[92] Each fighter jet or tank used to massacre Iraqi and Syrian civilians can instead cover student debt, tuition costs, fund social programs, entire schools, hospitals, or childcare facilities.[93] Instead, commercialized university administrations remain complicit in war crimes and illegal repression

---

[91] *The Struggle Inside. Prison Action Conference UC Berkley*

[92] *Solomon Amendment, 10 U.S.C. 983(b)(1)*

[93] *The Air War: The Myth of Deescalation. The Air War Action Committee*

through investments in military occupations, mass incarceration, recruitment for the military, FBI, and the CIA. In addition to military research that reduces the university to an ideological arm of imperialism that subordinates education to the needs of capitalism. Why reward the super-rich when they steal the natural resources from nations while punish the poor for expropriation to survive? Why criminalize the migration of those whom imperialism illegally displaces? Especially indigenous people that migrated naturally for centuries within their occupied homeland. What accounts for the absence of laws that prohibit corporations from the accumulation of billions in capital from businesses that "migrate" into other nations? Why an absence of tax laws to prohibit working class people from the duty to pay more taxes than the higher income? The foundation of the legal system fails to relinquish power to the majority with regards to the institutions that serve as the basis of the system designed to maintain unjust class and race relations between the exploiters and exploited, colonizer and colonized. These institutionalized inequities violate the basic human rights and liberties promised to the people by Western democracy. American imperialism that seeks to impose globally the repressive structures it enforces domestically warrants a worldwide unified struggle that uproots this injustice from the face of the earth with all injured parties justly compensated with reparations to redress the suffering.[94] [95]

Principle VI (Principle of Nuremberg Trials) The United States not only participated in the Nuremberg trials but held twelve additional trials after the initial international military tribunal. American judges participated with Francis Biddle as the primary judge. It has applied these principles domestically through US courts.[96]

---

[94] *A class action lawsuit by black farmers against the United States Department of Agriculture was settled by a consent decree, leading to nearly $1 billion in payments to plaintiffs. The lawsuit alleged systematic racial discrimination in the allocation of farm loans from 1981 to 1996. A further $1.2 billion was appropriated by Congress for the second part of the settlement. (The Pigford Cases, Congressional Research Service, May 29, 2013; see also Learning from the Germans: Race and the Memory of Evil by Susan Neiman (New York: Macmillan, 2019).)*

[95] *$105 million: Sioux of South Dakota for seizure of their land. (United States v. Sioux Nation of Indians,* **448 U.S. 371 (1980).)**

[96] *Abdullahi v. Pfizer, Inc.,* **562 F.3d 163 (2d Cir. 2009)**

The crimes hereinafter set out are punishable as crimes under international law. Crimes against peace:

i.   Planning, preparation, initiation or waging of a war of aggression or a war in violation of international treaties, agreements or assurances;

ii. Participation in a common plan or conspiracy for the accomplishment of any of the acts mentioned under (i).[97]

The United States Joint Chiefs of Staff first conspired Operation Cannon Bone[98] to militarily invade Syria and Iraq as early as 1958 and engaged in various forms of illegal warfare ever since.

Communication cables from the British embassy in Ankara[99] to Washington D.C. expressed urgent calls from Baghdad Pact members for American military invasion of Syria and Iraq to restore the monarchy and counter

---

[97] *82 U.N.T.S. 279*

[98] *Claudia Wright, "Generals' Assembly: The Secrets of US-Turkish Military Planning," New Statesmen (15 July 1983): 20.*

[99] *PO 371 / 133791 Sir John Baker. British Embassy in Ankara 1106. July 16 (Secret and Urgent)*

potential communist influence as well as anti-imperialist Arab nationalism. The day after the July 14 Revolution 1958 of Iraq the US Sixth Fleet sent troops to occupy Lebanon which marked the first American military invasion of the Arab region where the deadliest attack was inflicted on the US military in history by 1983 that forced them on the run. Meanwhile the British military invaded Jordan to try to contain the Iraqi Revolution. The CIA also conspired to "incapacitate" Colonel Fadhel Abbas al-Mahdawi after the July 14 Revolution of Iraq.[100]

By 1963 the US sponsored massacre that killed at least 15,000 alleged communists[101] comprised of Iraqi intellectuals, scientists, doctors, lawyers, professors, and

---

[100]   *Senate Select Committee to Study Governmental Operations with Respect to Intelligence Activities (Church Committee), Interim Report: Alleged Assassination Plots Involving Foreign Leaders, 94th Cong. 1st sess. (washington, DC: Government Printing Office, 1975), 181 n1. Testimony by CIA personnel indicated that the colonel for whom the handkerchief was intended later "[s]uffered a terminal illness before a firing squad in Baghdad."*

[101]   *Zeman W. J. & California State Polytechnic University Pomona. (2006). U.s. covert intervention in iraq 1958-1963 : the origins of u.s. supported regime change in modern iraq (dissertation). California State Polytechnic University Pomona.*

students amounts to one of the worst cold war massacres in history.[102] This was part of a counterinsurgency tactic adopted to "strengthen the capability of police and paramilitary organizations to counter communist inspired or exploited subversion and insurgency."[103] The lack of any accountability for these acts of aggression laid the groundwork for the overt invasion of Iraqi Republic and the subsequent war against the Syrian Arab Republic.

The U.S. was then complicit in the use of chemical weapons against Iranians[104] in an imposed war that caused the loss of over one million Iraqi and Iranian lives[105]

---

[102] *Nathan J. Citino, Envisioning the Arab Future: Modernization in U.S.–Arab Relations, 1945–1967, Global and International History (Cambridge: Cambridge University Press, 2017).*

[103] *National Security Action Memorandum No. 177, 7 August 1962, NSF, Robert W. Komer, box 413, Counterinsurgency; Police Program 1961-1963, Folder 3, JFKL; Rosenau, "The Kennedy Administration," 82-84, 97n128, 97n129*

[104] *UN failed to take action against Saddam for chemical weapons when he used them on behalf of the US but only raised issues when Iraq defied colonialism in a move towards the Soviet Union and against Sykes Picot; Kuwait 1991*

[105] *Taqi, J.M. (2008) 'Who Is More Worthy of Compensation: Iran or Iraq'. Ahewar, http://www.ahewar.org/ viewed*

after the Islamic Revolution in 1979.[106] Reports show that American helicopters used poisonous gas against Kurdish civilians in Iran. The Levant also was subject to proxy warfare in this period by various methods to undermine the Syrian Arab Republic. American client states in the region that commit human rights abuses with impunity with no oversight, in violation of the Leahy laws, work to destabilize Arab and Islamic nations free from the grip of neo-colonialism for reasons that include profits for oil monopolies and the American weapons industry.[107] The US led alliance in the region hence supported the insurrection of the Muslim Brotherhood through the supply of arms and explosives to undermine

---

[106] *The Institute for the Compilation and Publication of the Works of Imam Khomeinei. The Position of Women from the Viewpoint of Imam Khomeini.(2001)*

[107] *Hartung, William D. "Profits of War: Corporate Beneficiaries of the Post-9/11 Pentagon Spending Surge."*

the Syrian Arab Republic.[108] [109] This covert violation of Syrian sovereignty in 1982 coincided exactly with the direct military confrontation between the Syrian Arab Army and the Zionist, NATO, American invasion of Lebanon in the Battle of Sultan Yacoub, the Battle of Khalde, and various clashes that ultimately expelled the foreign forces.[110] That was after the Syrian government was formally invited by the Lebanese state unlike the Israeli occupation which breached the territorial integrity of Lebanon. The Zionist entity acts as the primary instrument of the United States that occupies the Arab region. The Mossad actively interfered in Iraqi affairs

---

[108] *Andre Gerolymatos "Castles Made of Sand: A Century of Anglo-American Espionage and Intervention in the Middle East" New York: St. Martin's Press, 2010, 347 pg. Western intelligence support for Muslim Brotherhood to subvert and undermine the Arab left and create an excuse for Anglo American intervention to stabilize the region*

[109] *Al-Hadaf. Editorial. PFLP Bulletin - April 1982 No. 61. Day of the Land p. 5*

[110] *Abed, Yaser. "Syrian Attack Helicopters." Syrian Tank-Hunters in Lebanon, 1982, Middle East Database, Sept. 2003, https://web. archive.org/web/20080321015417/http://www.acig.org/artman/ publish/article_279.shtml . **"Israeli Brigade suffered a loss of 18 - including its commander, Col. Avigdor Shriper - 87 injured, and 22 tanks destroyed."***

for decades alongside well documented CIA cooperation with the former Iranian SAVAK[111]. The Israelis attacked Iraq out of fear of the prospect of strengthened and more experienced militaries that threatened to redress the balance of forces with the Zionist entity.[112] Iraq launched missiles at the Israeli occupation in self-defense given the historic ties between Iraq and Palestine fortified by government of the July 14 Revolution.[113] The Zionists again bombed Iraq most recently on behalf of the US after the defeat of ISIS and continue to target Iraqi forces in the war on Syria as part of a genocidal effort to expand the Israeli occupation into Iraq.[114] [115]

[111] *Samii, "Role of SAVAK," 149-152; London A-2294 to State, March 8, 1967, RG59, CFPF 1967-1969, Box 2218*

[112] *Kadri, A. (2016). The Unmaking of Arab Socialism. Anthem Press. https://doi.org/10.2307/j.ctt1hj9zdb*

[113] *Palestine Liberation Army; We Will Return. Book found in Museum established by Iraqi Revolutionary Jawad al-Ta'i. Baghdad, Mutanabi Street. Iraqi Ministry of Justice. Iraq Public Law 106 http://www.iraqld.iq/LoadLawBook.aspx?SC=081120057960790*

[114] *Rubin, A. J. (2019, August 22). Israeli Airstrike Hits Weapons Depot in Iraq. New York Times. Retrieved September 1, 2022, from https://www.nytimes.com/2019/08/22/world/middleeast/israel-iraq-iran-airstrike.html*

[115] *See: Yinon Plan*

The US axis recruited mercenaries from over 90 countries to confiscate Syrian national independence. Both militarily and economically through coercive sanctions combined with the open theft of oil and wheat by foreign invasions in flagrant violation of the United Nations Charter.[116] [117] The US committed genocide to pollutes the most by its mass waste of stolen oil which causes environmental crises that compound the cataclysmic disaster across Iraq and Syria.[118] The primary polluter was a factor in the drought and dire conditions exploited for war on Syria as ecological calamities continue while America maintains the intolerable siege to suffocate the nation with the false impression of the contrary.

---

[116] *United Nations, Charter of the United Nations, 24 October 1945, 1 UNTS XVI*

[117] *China slams 'illegal' US troops, smuggling of oil, grain in Syria, 2022 WLNR 39061543*

[118] *Facing the Anthropocene: Fossil Capitalism and the Crisis of the Earth System, Ian Angus*

The Syrian & Iraqi Right To Self-Determination

The people of Iraq and Syria against extreme odds not only fight to reclaim their national resources, dignity, sovereignty, and independence but also defend the planet from mass extinction and ecological degradation.[119] Disproportionate US strikes against Syria and Iraq constitute war crimes and genocide against sovereign nations. Continued Syrian and Iraqi strikes on US forces[120] constitute self- defense against an illegal occupation in line with Article 51 of the UN Charter. In Iraq, this most recently forced Lockheed Martin to evacuate

---

[119] *Facing the Anthropocene: Fossil Capitalism and the Crisis of the Earth System, Ian Angus.*

[120] *US base in Syria's Koniko gas field comes under rocket attack "American forces injured in this attack" 1/5/23*

from Iraq[121] [122] and the US consulate to shut down in Basra[123] where the Iraqi masses disrupted Western oil production. Revolutionaries of Iraq & Syria struck US bases and obliterated their convoys throughout the past year in addition to a Zionist facility in northern Iraq[124]. The Syrian Arab Army recently shot down an Israeli jet just as it took down reconnaissance in the past as rockets continue to hit US bases which some reports indicate killed and injured several soldiers as recent as early fall of 2022.[125] [126] [127] The spokesman of Kata'ib Hezbollah

---

[121] ***Lockheed Martin, US contractor leaves Iraq base over rocket attacks***, *Agence France Presse (1991).*

[122] *US contractor leaves Iraq base over rocket attacks, 2021 WLNR 15282840*

[123] *National Iraqi News Agency, The US Embassy Closes Its Consulate In Basra For Security Reasons/ More, August 2, 2021.*

[124] *Mehr News Agency, Lexis®**10 Zionists killed, wounded in attack on Mossad HQ in Iraq** Lexis® - Sign In | LexisNexis (2021)*

[125] ***US Military Base in Syria Comes Under Intense Rocket Attack****: Reports, 2022 WLNR 29854091*

[126] *Rocket attacks in Syria injure 3 American service members*

[127] *US Troops Wounded in Rocket Attacks in Syria After US Airstrikes, 2022 WLNR 26773916*

declared that the occupation will find itself in the crosshairs of the Iraqi Resistance after the elimination of ISIS.[128] A victory achieved by the PMF and not America whose officials try to co-opt as their own. The Resistance Axis attacks against US bases[129] cut through the passive liberalism that dominates the US left and its response towards the events in Syria that ignores the high frequency of Zionist airstrikes. In prior years coalition soldiers fled from their bases southern Iraq.[130] The U.S. military suffered severe losses across Al-Anbar[131] most notably in Fallujah where they failed in their attempt to enter the

---

[128] *Jafar Al Husseini, Iraqi Hezbollah warns us against staying in country Home Page (2017), https://iblagh.com/en/iraqi-hezbollah-warns-us-staying-country/ (last visited May 20, 2018).* **The spokesman for the Iraq's Hezbollah Battalion said that the presence of Americans is more dangerous than Daesh terrorists as they have long-term plans for Iraq. Al-Hosseini warned the US forces against trying to stay in Iraq. "If Americans fail to leave Iraq, they will be in the crosshairs of the Iraqi Islamic resistance,"**

[129] *U.S. contractor dies in Iraq rocket attack, 2021 WLNR 7292913*

[130] *Militiamen 'take over Basra HQ', 2007 WLNR 26778724*

[131] *BLOODY OCTOBER US MILITARY DEATHS, 2006 WLNR 18895738* **Al-Anbar killed at at least 38 according to USA**

Senan Shaibani

Iraqi city. Diyala and all of Iraq evolved into highways of death for occupiers[132] to avenge for the US atrocity of 1991 known as the "the highway of death".[133] [134] The Iraqi masses defied the US led coalition despite how they faced a genocide rather than a war.

Figure 1: Iraqis celebrate the downing of U.S. helicopter, near Karbala

---

[132] *14 marines killed in Iraq bomb attack on armored vehicle, 2005 WLNR 12219165*

[133] *Robert H Reid & Anne Flaherty, Stryker Vehicle Losses Add Up Star News Onlin. 5 [US military vehicles] destroyed within a week in Diyala*

[134] *Black Hawk Helicopter destroyed and IEDs kill 20 US troops in Diala in single day*

International law affirms the right of people to resort to arms in their struggle for freedom.

On October 12, 1970, the United Nations General Assembly (Resolution 2621 (XXV)) affirmed that:

1. **Colonialism in all its forms and manifestations amounts to a crime that constitutes a violation of the charter of the United Nations, the resolution on the granting of independence to colonial nations and peoples, and violates the principles of international law.**

2. **Reaffirmed the inherent right of colonial peoples to struggle with all means at their disposal against the colonial power which suppresses their aspirations for liberty and independence.**[135]

Among the international documents which guarantee the right to self-determination and protect those who fight to exercise the right are:

• 1949 Geneva Convention

---

[135] *G.A. Res. 2621 (XXV), (1970).*

- Protocol Additional to the Geneva Conventions of 12 August 1949, and Relating to the Protection of Victims of International Armed Conflicts (Protocol I), June 8, 1977[136]

- Protocol Additional to the Geneva Conventions of 12 August 1949, and Relating to the Protection of Victims of Non-International Armed Conflicts (Protocol II), June 8, 1977[137]

- Universal Declaration of Human Rights[138]

- Gen. Assembly Resolution No. 217 (III), Dec. 10, 1948

- Convention on the Prevention and Punishment of the Crime of Genocide, Dec. 9, 1948[139]

- International Covenant on Civil and Political Rights, Dec. 16, 1966[140]

---

[136] *1125 U.N.T.S. 3.*

[137] *1125 U.N.T.S. 609.*

[138] *Universal Declaration of Human Rights, G.A. Res. 217A (III), U.N.G.A.O.R., 3rd Sess., Supp. No. 13, U.N. Doc. A/810 (1948) 71.*

[139] *78 U.N.T.S. 277.*

[140] *999 U.N.T.S. 171.*

Colonialism entails the imposition of political, economic, and social control by one nation over another. As this development accelerates the colonizer seeks to erase the colonized sense of identity by erasure of history, language, and culture. The armed struggle against Israeli colonialism was spearheaded by Izz al-Din al-Qassam[141] from the Syrian coastal town Jableh nearly a century ago. The Iraqi and Syrian people and Arab masses in general possess the right to take up arms to resist colonialism and liberate their lands. The right to struggle against imperialism judicially and other means through the domestic front also has legitimacy for the people of Syria, Iraq, and Palestine since neo- colonialism forced them from their homeland by wars for the violent theft of their natural wealth to serve as a cheap source of labor.[142] Self-determination and all forms of anti-colonial struggle for emancipation constitute the inherent and inalienable rights of nations and their peoples.[143]

---

[141] *Sayigh, Y. (1997). Armed Struggle and State Formation. Journal of Palestine Studies, 26(4), 17–32. https://doi.org/10.2307/2537904*

[142] *Al Shimari, et al. v. CACI*

[143] *Diplomatic Conference on Reaffirmation and Development of International Humanitarian Law Applicable to Armed Conflict*

Zionist aggression against Syria shows that the war against it belongs to the war on the Palestinian cause. The Syrian and Iraqi people who defend their homeland from an illegal occupation of mercenaries or conventional militaries exercise an inherent right to self-defense and self-determination enshrined by international law.[144] The Syrian allied forces that belong to Iraq expelled over 150,000 US troops in 2011 and other colonial forces in years prior through the exercise of the established right to liberate their nations from colonial invasion.[145] The Syrian Arab Republic and Iraqi Resistance proved to the people of the world that a determined struggle for independence will triumph against the United States[146]. A succession of American administrations all failed to stop the revolutionary fervor of anti- colonial struggle

---

[144] *IRAQI INSURGENTS DOWN HELICOPTER IN BAGHDAD KILLING CREW 2004 WLNR 2573368 "IRAQI MILITANT GROUP HOLDING 30 HOSTAGES INCLUDING AMERICANS AND ISRAELIS"*

[145] *U.S. Troops Leaving Iraq, Fulfilling Withdrawal Deadline Agreed to in 2008, 106 Am. J. Int'l L. 139 (2012)*

[146] *US Army Chief:Iraq War Has Sapped Ability to Fight Iran, Haaretz, 22 October 2007*

in the Levant and Iraq. Blockades, outright war, and various measures that cost trillions of U.S. dollars all failed which marks a victory that broadens the prospects of all marginalized people. To assess a loss or a victory requires one to examine whether the intended objectives succeed or fail in addition to the total cost The US federal government failed in the trillion-dollar effort to overthrow the Syrian government and implement a permanent occupation for a divided Iraq[147] severed from the Resistance Axis and the Palestinian cause. The steadfast nation of Iraq and Syria proves that all oppressed people possess the power to defeat the largest richest lawless organization in the world when united behind their just cause. Still the major victories await the region from the remainder of the illegal invasion and the resolution of internal contradictions.

The Universal Declaration of the Rights of People ("Algiers Declaration") declares that oppressed people" have an equal right to liberty, the right to free themselves from any foreign interference and to choose their own government, (and) the right, if they are under subjection,

---

[147] ***Sen. Biden:Divide Iraq into Three Regions"***

to fight for their liberation."[148] This was specified in Article 1: "Every people has the right to existence," and Article 6: "Every people has the right to break free from any colonial or foreign domination, whether direct or indirect, and from any racist regime." U.N. Resolution 2625 (XXV) or "The Declaration on the Principles of International Law Concerning Friendly Relations and Co-Operation Among States in Accordance with the Charter of the United Nations" clarifies the nature and significance of the right to self-determination.[149] The resolution states "the principle of equal rights and self-determination of peoples

---

[148] *Declaration of the Government of the Democratic and Popular Republic of Algeria Concerning the Settlement of Claims by the Government of the United States of America and the Government of the Islamic Republic of Iran (Jan. 19, 1981), https://jusmundi. com/en/document/treaty/en-declaration-of-the-government-of-the-democratic-and-popular-republic-of- algeria-concerning-the-settlement-of-claims-by-the-government-of-the-united-states-of-america-and-the-government-of-the- islamic-republic-of-iran-claims-settlement-declaration-1981-algiers-declaration-claims-settlement-1981-monday-19th- january-1981.*

[149] *Verdict of the Special International Tribunal on the Violation of Human Rights of Political Prisoners and Prisoners of Wars in United States Prisons and Jails.*

constitutes a significant contribution to contemporary law."[150]

Despite the victories won by the Iraqi people great turmoil still exists in the nation. Americans cause much of the strife by attempts to hold onto control over the state apparatus. The defeat of the U.S. occupation achieved by the Iraqi Resistance forced the invaders to retreat out of from the public that captured, sniped, and incinerated them. The few that remain fled to hide in the remote fortified bases disguised as a diplomatic mission yet still in the line of fire by missiles, bullets, and drones. From these illegal bases that serve as crucibles of torture, espionage, supply lines, logistical support, geopolitical influence, and components of war plans, they devise the policy of arms transfers to local sell outs to carry out counter revolutionary wars on their behalf. Iraq always stood as a revolutionary nation that struggled for liberation from the grip of imperialism which now imposes extremes of

---

[150] *Declaration of the Principles of International Law Concerning Friendly Relations and Cooperation Among States in Accordance with the Charter of the United Nations, G.A. Res. 2708(XXV), U.N. GAOR, 25th Sess., Suppl. no.28, U.N. Doc. A/RES/2708(XXV).*

poverty and wealth, corruption, and repression. The neo-colonial state has independence only theoretically.

The internal politics and economy remain dictated externally in a variety of ways. The soldiers of neo-colonial power preserve the state and control the political establishment. The situation in Iraq resembles a degree of neo-colonialism despite the retreat of occupation forces.[151] The invasion of Iraq tried to establish a sectarian political system subordinate to the U.S. regime.[152] So called U.S. military 'advisors' and contractors oversee crimes committed against the Iraqi people yet continue to sell the weapons that kill them. If the national military depends on outsiders for weapons, advisors, training, and support then those outsiders control the military. The US tried to appeal to Iraqi Shia as part of their agenda[153] whose masses strongly reject their sectarian order and recognize the reality of the American plan that suggests "Iraqi Shia

---

[151] *BRITAIN TO PULL ALL TROOPS FROM IRAQ. San Jose Mercury News (CA)12.18. 2008. Clashes with Shi'ite Militas*

[152] *Soren Scholvin, The Failure Of Nation-Building in Iraq, 15 THE JOURNAL OF INTERNATIONAL ISSUES 48 (2011).*

[153] *Paul Bremer Plans for Iraq*

do whatever you want on condition that you never support Palestine and claim ownership of your oil and national wealth."[154] Not a single religious authority in Iraq, especially in Najaf, will provide the occupation with cover to cooperate with it. Iraqi Sunnis comprised of nationalists valiantly made life especially unbearable for the coalition but as the movement was infiltrated by foreign sectarianism the Iraqi Shia continued the defiant legacy and Sunni Arabs and Kurds joined their ranks.

"The truth is that most of our kids that have been killed have been killed by extremist Shi'ite groups not by Al-Qaeda in Iraq" – Robert Gates former secretary of defense

"Our highest number of U.S. soldiers killed in Iraq were killed by Kata'ib Hezbollah, Asa'ib al Haqq, or the Promised Day Brigade" – U.S. general

"Iran is providing material support for attacks on American troops. We will disrupt the attacks on our forces. We will interrupt the flow from Iran and Syria that

---

[154] *The Voice of Hezbollah. Transcripts of Sayyed Hassan Nasrallah speeches*

provide advance weaponry and training to our enemies in Iraq" – George Bush[155]

"This series of outcomes make the invasion [Iraq] a fiasco without parallel since Vietnam and without end in sight" – U.S. foreign officer

They expected the people of Iraq to welcome them with open arms instead of fight back with weapons, martyrdom operations, missiles, and improvised explosive devices by revolutionary armies that now transfer weapons to Palestine and stand prepared to combat the Zionist entity as they continue their protracted struggle. Iraqi revolutionaries gained battle experience throughout their struggle that proved instrumental in assistance to the Syrian Arab Republic in the defeat of US proxies.

---

[155] *Interview on NBC's Today Show With Matt Lauer, U.S. Department of State, (Jan. 11, 2007) https://2001*

Figure 2: Hundreds of deadly attacks on US convoys and bases in Iraq 2021[156] [157]

However, the undivided vote by the Iraq for the expulsion of all US military after the extrajudicial murder of General Qasim Soleimani and Hajj Abu Mahdi al-Muhandis[158] was not respected by the US in blatant violation of internationally recognized norms. *Article 2.4 demands that all UN Charter members avoid threats or use of force that violate the territorial integrity or*

[156] *Infographic: Iraqi resistance groups operations against the US in 2021, Islamic World News (2021), https://english.iswnews. com/22129/infographic-iraqi-resistance-groups-operations-against-the-us-in-2021/ (last visited Mar 14, 2021).*

[157] *Iraq: Attacks on Western targets. 4/15/21. US Embassy stormed and US & UK troops killed. Agence Fr.-Presse 09:51:43*

[158] *Iraqi Parliament Votes To Expel U.S. Troops, Trump Threatens Sanctions, NPR, (Jan. 6, 2020) https://www.npr. org/2020/01/06/793895401/iraqi-parliament-votes-to-expel-u-s-troops-trump-threatens-sanctions.*

political independence of any state159. The murder of General Qasim Soleimani, Hajj Abu Mahdi al-Muhandis, Muhammad Shaibani, among other Iraqi Mujahideen at a time of peace via drone that disrupted a diplomatic mission was another breach of international humanitarian and human rights law. This assault against Iraqi leadership and an invited state official violates Iraqi sovereignty and constitutes a crime against humanity that the International Criminal Court has the jurisdiction to prosecute.[160] The attack against the leaders of the movement that defeated the American Caliphate (ISIS) amounts to an unlawful act of aggression and crime against peace pursuant to UN General Assembly Resolution 3314.[161] State sanctioned murder of this kind that American presidents take credit for makes them liable to criminal indictment. It constitutes a lawless denial to the right to life enshrined

---

[159] *U.N. Charter art. 4, 2.*

[160] *Assassination of Gen Soleimani, violation of int'l law: US expert "breach of JCPOA"*

[161] *G.A. Res. 3114 (XXIX).*

by Article 6 and 14 of the International Covenant on Civil and Political Rights[162].

Principle V (Nuremberg Trial)

Any person charged with a crime under international law has the right to a fair trial on the facts and law.

Neo-colonial transgressions extend to cyber warfare, mass media campaigns, academia, missionaries, pacification by low intensity warfare, and economic measures that obstruct the development of the sovereign will and political consciousness of post-colonial nation states. The United States government violated its own constitutional principles that protects the freedom of the press when it seized Iraqi websites as part of a cyber campaign for political censorship.[163] The descendants of the greatest scientists in history who discovered algorithms, now misused by neocolonialism, still manage to engage in cyber defense despite all odds. Iraqi cyber resistance

---

[162] *999 U.N.T.S. 171.*

[163] *US blocks Iraq militia websites after the group stormed the US Embassy in Baghdad, 2021 WLNR 9981951*

shuts down Israeli websites in retaliation, disables siren alarms to alert rocket attacks to defend Palestine, hacks into the personal devices of the chief of the Mossad, closed major American oil pipelines in Iraq which raised crude prices in West Texas, hacks into US drones, and employs a diverse set of tactics to frustrate neo-colonial schemes and plans[164]. The Syrian Electronic Resistance likewise has penetrated the Pentagon to gather intelligence and broadcast the name Hezbollah throughout the monitors within the facility.[165]

Neo-colonial power demands that states take production techniques and manufactured products such as weapons produced by Lockheed Martin to the exclusion of competitive products from Russia and other markets.[166] The colonial government and U.S. corporations such as

---

[164] ***Oil prices are rising after a cyber attack caused the closure of important American pipelines****. National Iraqi News Agency (NINA). Provided by SyndiGate Media Inc. May 10, 2021*

[165] *Hezbollah took over Pentagon RT. Retrieved 10, 2019, https://www. rt.com/news/470408-hezbollah-take-over-pentagon/*

[166] *Team, E. (2020, December 13). **US warns Iraq of sanctions, if it buys Russian military equipment**. Anti-Interventionist Movement. Retrieved 2021, from https://thatsenough.info/?p=605*

Halliburton conspire to monopolize oil reservoirs and impose illegal military bases where private contractors provide services to the war effort in extraction of natural resources.[167] [168] [169] Government strategy in neo-colonial states seeks to secure itself by payments towards the value of state rule, through civil servants such as Mohammed Shia al Sudani based in the Green Zone[170]where they direct policy in line with colonial designs, and by monetary authority over foreign trade through the banks controlled by the United States. Where neo-colonialism exists the power that reigns constitutes the bourgeoisie state which once ruled the land in question.[171] For example, in Iraq the former imperial power was Britain, but the Iraqi

---

[167] *EXCLUSIVE-**Attacks on major Iraqi gasfield drive out U.S. contractors** August 30,2022*

[168] *Drone attacks on Saudi Arabia from Iraq are a new threat, 2021 WLNR 5727981*

[169] ***Five missiles fired at Halliburton in Iraq,*** *say Iranian media, 2020 WLNR 13360122*

[170] *Shooting reported at US military base in Iraq's Green Zone December 14 2022*

[171] *Sbahi, A. (2018), 'The Communist Party's activities among the peasantry', International Journal of Contemporary Iraqi Studies, 12:2, pp. 111–26, doi: 10.1386/jcis.12.2.111_1*

Senan Shaibani

Revolution overthrew the western client state in the wake of WWII and established anti-colonial political power that continues today in the Popular Mobilization Forces[172]. The Iraqi people stood united against the American occupation to demand a timetable for the end of their combat mission which faced efficient military operations until the popular will left them with no option but to respect the demand.[173] The highest judiciary of Iraq has also issued an arrest warrant for Donald Trump who will face prosecution if he travels to Iraq with the knowledge of authorities.[174] Unlike like when he illegally crossed the Iraqi border secretly due to the Iraqi insurgency that the US-led coalition failed to liquidate.

[172] *British troops flee rockets blitz on base, 2021 WLNR 7148751*

[173] *War in Iraq was mistake', 2007 WLNR 17273009*

[174] *Iraq confirms arrest warrant issued for Trump over militia leaders death*

Figure 3: A revolutionary Iraqi woman in a mass demonstration against the French occupation of Syria in the 1930s.

The minister of social affairs Dr. Kinda al Shammat[175] whom remains restricted by the US regime announced the establishment of women & children in cooperation with the UNHCR and legislation to combat rape, honor killing, human trafficking (the capital in US), as Syria has membership in international treaties on the rights of women in the struggle against discrimination. Lubana Mshawweh works as a Syrian woman in a government leadership position who was besieged by the US. Maysa' Salih

---

[175] *Government Stresses On Protection of Women and Children in Wartime. Syrian Arab News Agency. 12/1/14*

holds another government leadership position in the scientific studies and research center that was bombed by the Trump regime. Buthaina Shaaban who works as a high ranked official and special advisor to the presidency represents another Syrian woman in a leadership position beseiged by the US government.

The occupation also presented itself as the liberation of Iraqi women whose situation only deteriorated since the invasion.[176] The United States counts as one of the only nations that has not ratified the **Convention on the Elimination of all Forms of Discrimination Against Women**[177] or the **Convention on the Rights of the Child**[178]. Raghad Sarraj who serves as the chairwoman of the Iraqi Students Office in Syria pointed out 2,000

---

[176] *Al-Ali, Nadje, and Nicola Pratt. What Kind of Liberation?: Women and the Occupation of Iraq. 1st ed. University of California Press, 2009. http://www.jstor.org/stable/10.1525/j.ctt1pnft4.*

[177] *1249 U.N.T.S. 13.*

[178] *1577 U.N.T.S. 3.*

confirmed rape cases committed by US occupation forces[179] whose victims include minors and the elderly. The Resistance Forum for Women[180] organized by Arab women highlighted the role of the Resistance Axis against the decadent colonialism that promotes racist tropes about the need to save Arab and Muslim women from the stereotypical terrorist caricature. This kind of propaganda tries to build public support for US led wars in a region where America hypocritically supports autocratic regimes and factions that restrict and violate the rights of women.[181] The Syrian constitution of 1973 which resembled the Iraqi constitution established that "the state guarantees women all opportunities enabling them to participate in political, social, cultural, and economic life fully and effectively. The state removes the restrictions that prevent

---

[179] *Ismael, M. (May 28, 2012) Resistance Women Forum Expresses Standing by Syria against Conspiracy. Syrian Arab News Agency. https://plus.lexis.com/document/?pdmfid=1530671&crid=7904 75b6-048a-415f-b996- fa8223ee5e93&pddocfullpath=%2Fsh ared%2Fdocument%2Fnews%2Furn%3AcontentItem%3A55RT-CGX1-JDJN-62DB- 00000-00&pdcontentcomponentid=35695 4&pdteaserkey=&pdislpamode=false&pdworkfolderlocatorid= 8500126c-f8fb- 4022-ad7d-9d19046ad98d&ecomp=bfbtk&earg =sr0&prid=16a77a00-f93d-4d0d-9a14-c0d975398d5e*

[180] *Id.*

[181] *Hollywood's Anti-Arab and Anti-Muslim Propaganda, 2015 WLNR 3343224 "killing women and children inevitable" Palestine News Network*

the development of women and their participation in building the socialist Arab society".[182] The July 14th Revolution of Iraq expanded the freedom of women in their political rights when the British imposed monarchy was dismantled.[183] Naziha al-Dulaymi was the leader of the Iraqi League for the Defense of Women and first female cabinet member in the entire Arab region whom contributed to the passage of Public Law 180 that improved the status of women vastly after the overthrow of colonialism.[184] Naziha al-Dulaymi oversaw the construction of Revolution City with public projects for the underprivileged of Baghdad which later served as a site of intense urban clashes spearheaded by the Mahdi Army against coalition troops and neo-colonial garrisons.[185] [186] [187]

---

[182] *Syria – Constitution Adopted on 13 March 1873 http://www.servat. unibe.cn/icl/su00000_.html (viewed 20 November 2022)*

[183] *Albert, Richard, Menaka Guruswamy, and Nishchal Basnyat. Founding Moments in Constitutionalism. Ed. Richard Albert, Menaka Guruswamy, and Nishchal Basnyat. Oxford, UK: Hart Publishing, 2019. Print.*

[184] *Iraqi Judge Kashkul, Hasan. Interpretation of the Civil Status Law 188 of 1958. Ministry of Justice Iraqi Law Records*

[185] *Americans targeted in Sadr City, 2008 WLNR 11875774*

[186] *ON A BLOODY DAY IN SADR CITY, U.S., IRAQI SOLDIERS ENGAGE MILITIAS IN STREETS, 2008 WLNR 7982479*

[187] *U.S. Troops Killed as Fighting Reignites in Sadr City, 2008 WLNR 6512878*

The Anglo-American imperialism has attempted to recolonize the Iraqi Republic through various forms of warfare. Likewise, in Syria the previous colonial power was France, until it was driven out by a diverse coalition that represents the pluralism that the United States and NATO allies actively seek to recolonize and partition. A state in the grip of neo-colonialism will never achieve an independent national, political, economic, and social destiny.[188] This makes neo-colonialism a form of enslavement imposed on colonized nations which undermines harmonious relations amongst humankind.

Nevertheless, the American project for the "New Middle East" failed to divide Iraq[189] and dismantle the Syrian Arab Republic: an ominous declaration to the US federal government and a source of motivation for the downtrodden of the world that suffer grave hardships

---

[188] *Kwame Nkrumah, Neo-Colonialism, The Last Stage of Imperialism; First Published: in 1965 by Thomas Nelson & Sons, Ltd., London. Published in the USA by International Publishers Co., Inc., 1966;*

[189] *Houston National Public Library (2006, September 29). **Sen. Biden: Divide Iraq into Three Regions**. NPR. Retrieved December 22, 2022, from https://www.npr.org/2006/09/29/6166796/sen-biden-divide-iraq-into-three-regions*

under this global status quo. The Popular Mobilization Forces defeated the American Caliphate (ISIS) in less than three years despite claims by the CIA of a war for thirty years with the aim of corporate profits and a weakened resistance movement after the mass retreat of the military combat invasion from Iraq. The Iraqi and Syrian defeat of ISIS constitutes a defeat of U.S. imperialism that produced it. Israeli attacks prove that the U.S. military power failed to defeat a struggle for independence in Iraq. It indicates that a political force in Iraq still poses a major threat to the colonization of the Arab nation.[190]

"Whereas it is essential, if man is not to be compelled to have recourse, as a last resort, to rebellion against tyranny and oppression, that human rights should be protected by the rule of law ..."
- Preamble to the Universal Declaration of Human Rights, December 10, 1948

---

[190] *Jonathan Spyer, The growing threat facing Israel from Iraq The Jerusalem Post | JPost.com (2021), https://www.jpost.com/middle-east/the-growing-threat-facing-israel-from-iraq-670071 (last visited Feb 13, 2022).*

Indictment Of The U.S. Federal Government

The Preamble to the Universal Declaration of Human Rights states that each state has a duty to advance self-determination and to aid the United Nations for improved relations amongst states "to bring a speedy end to colonialism, having due regard to the freely expressed will of the peoples concerned."[191] The right of self-determination as a major principle of international law was declared by the International Court of Justice in the *Advisory Opinion on Namibia (ICJ Reports 1971)*[192] and in the decision in *the Western Sahara case (ICJ Reports 1975)*[193]. As the *Vienna Convention on the Law of Treaties* asserts, no action of sovereign determination or agreement can replace it.[194] The two international agreements on human rights *International Covenant on Economic, Social, and Cultural Rights* and *International Covenant on Civil and Political Rights* (which the United States has refused to sign on to) started by a common Article 1(1) that indicates a place of primacy for self-determination: "All

---

[191] *G.A. Res. 217A (III), U.N. Doc. A/810 at 71 (1948).*

[192] *Diggs v. Richardson,* **555 F.2d 848 (D.C. Cir. 1976)**

[193] *Zarouite v. Gonzales,* **424 F.3d 60 (1ˢᵗ Cir. 2005)**

[194] *1155 U.N.T.S. 331.*

75

peoples have the right of self-determination. By virtue of that right they freely determine their political status and freely pursue their economic, social, and cultural development".[195]For this decolonial process to take full force it will require a strong united front lead by the most committed revolutionary leadership that shows the masses the power they possess through their political organization that rejects capitulation.

---

[195] *993 U.N.T.S. 3; 999 U.N.T.S. 171.*

Political Repression, Subversion, Criminalization

The past several US administrations went to war against Syria and Iraq without declaration by the US Congress which constitutes the only agency with the power to declare war that last transpired in 1942. The offensive use of the US military that started with Iraq was declared illegal by the United Nations Security Council.[196] The use of force without UN authorization establishes a dangerous precedent and great risk for nations of the world. While the US launched the war on Iraq - with the failure to garner support from African countries on the Security Council - the Bush administration moved to cripple the legally elected government of Zimbabwe which

---

[196] *The United Nations secretary general, Kofi Annan, declared explicitly that the US-led war on Iraq was illegal.*

demonstrates worldwide imperialist plans beyond the so called "war on terror".[197]

A state violates international law when it criminalizes the struggle of nations and peoples to attain self-determination. Pursuant to the **Declaration of the Principles of International Law Concerning Friendly Relations and Cooperation Among States in Accordance with the Charter of the United Nations:** "Every State has the duty to refrain from any forcible action which deprives peoples ... of their right to self-determination and freedom and independence"[198] in addition to Resolutions 33/22 and 33/24 (1978) which repudiate the incarceration of people who struggle against colonialism. Therefore, the designation of national liberation movements indigenous to Syria and Iraq as "terrorist" or "state sponsors of terrorism" violates the

---

[197] *Mr. Tirivafi Kangai Statement to the UN Decolonization Committee (Zimbabwe). Zimbabwe African National Union*

[198] *Declaration of the Principles of International Law Concerning Friendly Relations and Cooperation Among States in Accordance with the Charter of the United Nations, G.A. Res. 2708(XXV), U.N. GAOR, 25ᵗʰ Sess., Suppl. no.28, U.N. Doc. A/RES/2708(XXV), at 122.*

inherent right for oppressed nations to self-determination. American conspiracy legislation criminalizes political anti-imperialism. It seeks to criminalize popular resistance and sidesteps the US role in the inception of "terrorism" to delegitimize national liberation movements and provide a pretext for US military intervention in revolutionary societies so that client regimes build on their ruins.[199]

The US wrongfully convicted the Holy Land 5 for "material support to terrorism" with life imprisonment for distribution of humanitarian aid to Palestine.[200] [201] Representatives of the United States deserve that conviction, not the Holy Land 5, for American "material support to terrorism" to foreign forces guilty of human rights abuses

---

[199] *Glen Ford & 11 Jul 2013, THE U.S. WAR AGAINST THE WORLD BLACK AGENDA REPORT (2013), https://blackagendareport. com/content/us-war-against-world (last visited Jan 9, 2023).*

[200] *Boim v. Holy Land Found. for Relief & Dev., 549 F.3d 685 (7ᵗʰ Cir. 2008)*

[201] *Saikrishna B. Prakash & Michael D. Ramsey, The Executive Power over Foreign Affairs, 111 Yale L.J. 231 (2001) "the President cannot regulate international commerce" this raises the question of the constitutionality of the International Emergency Economic Powers Act as George Bush disrupted humanitarian aid to Palestine with no constitutional basis.*

in Syria, Iraq, Palestine, Yemen, and abroad. This US financial support also violates the Leahy amendments through ties to fascist entities such as the Saudi monarchy whose petrodollars propagates the ideology of "terrorist" movements.[202] This demonstrates how the US federal government employs the language of national security as a cover to push for repressive measures through the development of a despotic police state domestically and military and economic aggression internationally. Yet instead of any substantial effort to place US officials on trial for these extreme and outrageous crimes, Muslims who allegedly attempt to alleviate the disastrous conditions caused by said violations face severe charges and convictions.[203] The American war against Islam has no comparison in scale since the height of the cold war as stated by US officials. Expert eyewitnesses indigenous to Iraq and Syria will testify that CIA covert operatives infiltrate if not manufacture organizations that commit war crimes and absolve the U.S. political establishment

---

[202] *22 U.S.C. § 2378d; 10 U.S.C. § 362.*

[203] *USA, v. HOLY LAND FOUNDATION FOR RELIEF AND DEVELOPMENT et al., 2004 WL 5031836*

of culpability.[204] US military generals and officials at the Pentagon need to face justice for both overt and covert attacks against sacred mosques and other historic sites across Iraq, Syria, and Palestine.[205] **Article 53**[206] **Protection of cultural objects and places of worship without prejudice to the provisions of The Hague Convention for the Protection of Cultural Property in the Event of Armed Conflict of 14 May 1954, and of other relevant international instruments, prohibits:**

> **(a.) to commit any acts of hostility directed against the historic monuments, works of art or places of worship which constitute the cultural or spiritual heritage of peoples.**

The pentagon conducts psychological military operations in the name of Islam that promote violent

---

[204] *Testimony from majority of Iraqi civilians and soldiers when I resided in Baqubah for one year*

[205] ***US-led coalition strikes mosque in eastern Syria.** 10/22/18 Anadolu Agency (Turk.) 20:10:46. WestLaw*

[206] *Protocol 1 Additional to the Geneva Conventions, 1977 Part 5: Article 54*

sectarianism such as the attack on the shrine of Imam Muhammad al-Hadi (AS) sacred to Shi'ite Muslims or the execution of Saddam Hussein on Eid al-Adha in the Sunni Muslim calendar. These efforts seek to try to prevent what emerged in the first battle of Fallujah when Sunni and Shi'i Iraqi insurgents joined forces organically as they coexisted historically and defeated the US military[207] whose invasion of Iraq injected the venom of sectarianism to partition the pluralistic nation as Biden advocated.

---

[207] *Reuters, "August 21, 2004." Muqtada. Patrick Cockburn*

Figure 4: Infamous Fallujah bridge where justice was served to American contractors in the absence of UN action

Locals in the Iraqi village of Buhriz testified that Al Qaeda infiltrators executed members of the national liberation movement who shot down a US helicopter over the Sunni village.[208] [209] The US funded and armed "terrorism" in Syria and then invaded in the name of the "war on terror" when they saw the Syrian Arab Army and Hezbollah advance against it.[210] The U.S. federal government claims to fight the "terrorism" it sponsored as a pretext to reinvade Iraq and occupy Syria to seize the oil rich territories in the northeastern region where U.S. forces continue to openly steal Syrian fuel. The U.S. exploited their "terrorist" armies of mercenaries for a decade now with the failed objective to eradicate the Axis of Resistance and as an excuse to remain in Iraq and Syria indefinitely.[211] To under develop and delete from the regional formula revolutionary nations that

---

[208] *1ST LEAD: **Another US helicopter down [Baqubah], British bases bombed.***

[209] *Iraqi National Resistance Archive. Anonymous Eye Witness. 1/28/2018*

[210] *Maté, A. (2022, April 23). 'Al Qaeda is on our side': How Obama/ Biden team empowered terrorist networks in Syria. MR Online. Retrieved October 17, 2022, from https://mronline.org/2022/04/23/ al-qaeda-is-on-our-side/*

[211] *Taylor, G. (2017, January 10). Obama hoped to use ISIS as leverage against Assad, John Kerry reveals. The Washington Times. Retrieved October 19, 2022, from https://mronline.org/2022/04/23/ al-qaeda-is-on-our-side/*

oppose Zionism and imperialism so that America may emerge as the self-proclaimed Western colonial savior. U.S. and Zionist air raids continue to target the Syrian Arab Army, Hezbollah, Iraqi revolutionary forces, and the IRGC whenever they successfully move against ISIS and its offshoots without the help of the Western culprits.[212] [213] [214]Israeli hospitals provided treatment to Al-Qaeda and opposition fighters throughout the war as their warplanes target the Resistance Axis with unlimited

---

[212] ***Israel responds to Syrian Army advance against ISIS in Deir Ezzor, strikes Syrian military*** *facility in Masyaf, South Front (2017), https://southfront.org/israel-responds-to-syrian-army-advance-against-isis-in-deir-ezzor-strikes-syrian-military-facility-in-masyaf/ (last visited Feb 9, 2018).*

[213] *Brandon Turbeville,* ***U.S. attacks Syrian military, protects Isis*** *Renegade Tribune (2016), http://www.renegadetribune.com/**u-s-attacks-syrian-military-protects-isis**/ (last visited Oct 15, 2022).*

[214] *John Wright,* ***Israel's giving Isis an air force*** *The Iran Project (2017), https://theiranproject.com/blog/2017/08/30/israels- giving-isis-air-force/ (last visited Jul 29, 2021).*

American support.[215] Repeated Israeli violations of UNSC Resolution 350 of 1974 take the lives of Syrian children with immunity from penalties by Western Security Council Members. Various factions identical to ISIS sponsored by the CIA clashed with those established by the Pentagon.[216] The US regime engages in unauthorized military action in violation of Iraqi and Syrian sovereignty where it failed through unlawful covert means by proxy warfare. The U.S. sponsored "terrorism" as an attempt to sabotage and weaken the resistance movement that expelled U.S. troops from Iraq. The American regime laid a trap for Al-Qaeda in Syria. The most impactful patriotic voice I heard in Syria where I resided in 2017 was from an internally displaced Syrian from Idlib who expressed his

---

[215] *https://www.huffpost.com/entry/fighting-between-the-pent_b_9609308 (last visited May 14, 2017). JPOST STAFF, Report: Israel treating Al-Qaida fighters wounded in Syria Civil War The Jerusalem Post | JPost.com (2015), https://www.jpost.com/middle-east/report-israel-treating-al-qaida-fighters-wounded-in-syria-civil-war-393862 (last visited Apr 9, 2015).*

[216] *David Oualalou, FIGHTING BETWEEN THE PENTAGON AND CIA-BACKED MILITIAS PORTRAYS A CHAOTIC U.S. FOREIGN POLICY HUFFPOST (2017), https://www.huffpost.com/entry/fighting-between-the-pent_b_9609308 (last visited May 14, 2017).*

allegiance to President Assad and the Syrian Arab Army with outrage over the murder of his son by Al Qaeda militias that still occupy the city.[217] These efforts seek to divide and prevent the non-compliant nations of Iraq and Syria from cohesion and control of their own politics that dictates their own economies and societies.

This tactic also has domestic implications aimed at the repression, sabotage, infiltration, entrapment, raids, harassment, and massive FBI surveillance of the diaspora and solidarity movements with the curtailment of civil liberties.[218] "Terrorism" as used by the U.S. federal government subverts fundamental rights to make the legal system function as a form of counter insurgency that denies fair trials by impartial juries with defendants detained indefinitely without charge under conditions that violate principles of the *United Nations Standard*

---

[217] *Internally displaced Syrian from Idlib interviewed in Damascus*

[218] *Poirot, Collin. "The Anatomy of a Federal Terrorism Prosecution: A Blueprint for Repression and Entrapment." Columbia Human Rights Law Review, 8 Dec. 2020, pp. 61–96.*

Minimum Rules for the Treatment of Prisoners.[219] The US regime undermines basic democratic rights and constitutional principles to prevent organized opposition against violations of international law committed by the US government. This requires revolutionary legal support to make the system conform to its own stated principles as achieved in *Handschu v. Special Services Div.*, 273 F. Supp. 2d 327 (S.D.N.Y. 2003). This case was won with the support of mass struggle in conjunction with the legal struggle to rally the public to apply pressure against the court against covert tactics by the state. *Handschu* demonstrates the crucial capacity for legal assistance to make the system adhere to its proclaimed principles of liberty and justice despite the inherent defects with the constitution and legal system itself. The colonial "justice" system never admits to guilt without a committed struggle with popular support that forces the state to bend and make concessions.

---

[219] *UN General Assembly, United Nations Standard Minimum Rules for the Treatment of Prisoners (the Nelson Mandela Rules): resolution / adopted by the General Assembly, 8 January 2016, A/RES/70/175, available at: https://www.refworld.org/docid/5698a3a44.html*

The term "terrorism" warrants criticism because it lacks an internationally recognized definition and consensus.[220] Decades prior to the September 11 attacks, the United States developed "Alien Terrorists and Undesirables: A Contingency Plan" to place Arabs and Muslims from Syria and other countries across the region in concentration camps.[221] The state of emergency declared by George H. W. Bush who vetoed the 1990 Civil Rights Bill granted him the authority to detain Iraqi or any Arab people in the name of "national security".[222] The secret contingency plan that outlined preparations for the mass detention of Arabs and Muslims in the U.S. was leaked and thus the project was withheld in the face of resistance from community organizations and legal

---

[220] *Syria's President Assad issues general amnesty for terror-related crimes, 2022 WLNR 4137397*

[221] *Ben Wofford, The Forgotten Government Plan to Round Up Muslims, POLITICO, (Aug. 19, 2016) https://www.politico.com/magazine/story/2016/08/secret-plans-detention-internment-camps-1980s-deportation-arab-muslim- immigrants-214177/.*

[222] *See George W. Bush, Declaration of National Emergency by Reason of Certain Terrorist Attacks, THE WHITE HOUSE: OFFICE OF THE PRESS SECRETARY, (Sept. 14, 2001) https://georgewbush-whitehouse.archives.gov/news/releases/2001/09/20010914-4.html.*

associations long before the establishment of Guantanamo Bay. The FBI and U.S. law enforcement nonetheless still harassed and interrogated 200 Arab community leaders weekly throughout the country rather than take any action to prevent racist attacks on Muslims that anti-Iraqi propaganda motivated as missiles massacred hundreds of thousands of Arabs in 1991.[223]

<u>Art. 8 of the Universal Declaration of Human Rights:[224] "everyone ("aliens" and nationals co-equal) has the right to an effective remedy by the competent national tribunals for acts violating the fundamental rights granted to him by the constitution or by the law</u>"[225].

Anwar al-Awlaki was assassinated by drone[226] with his young children each killed separately in complete disregard for due process of the fifth amendment of

---

[223] *Government Attacks and Violence Against Arab People. Neal Saed.*

[224] *Universal Declaration of Human Rights, 1948, art. 8*

[225] *G.A. Res. 217A (III), U.N. Doc. A/810 at 71 (1948).*

[226] *Drone Strike That Killed Awlaki "Did Not Silence Him," Journalist Says, NPR, (Sept. 14, 2015) https://www.npr.org/2015/09/14/440215976/journalist-says-the-drone-strike-that-killed-awlaki-did-not-silence-him.*

the US constitution, presumption of innocence, the Nuremberg Trials, and the International Covenant on Civil and Political Rights. Guilty, convicted and sentenced to capital punishment. The murder violated precedent set by **Reid v. Covert**, 354 U.S. 1 (1956)[227] which stated that constitutional protections awarded to US citizens remain intact in foreign countries, without subjection to military jurisdiction. Awlaki first incurred FBI harassment for his condemnation of the crimes against Iraq. If the White House justifies the murder of an Arab child as a descendant of Al-Qaeda then what penalty will redress the descendance from white supremacists guilty of genocide and slavery? Even this analogy fails to demonstrate the degree of injustice committed against children who remain innocent until proven guilty unlike the White House which legitimate trials proved guilty of past and continued crimes of severe magnitude. In his time as Senator in support of war on Iraq, Vice President at the time of the murder of the Awlakis and war on Syria, and the administration of the illegitimate Presidency of the United States, Joseph Robinette Biden Jr. has

---

[227] *Reid v. Covert, 351 U.S. 487, 76 S. Ct. 880 (1956)*

violated his responsibility to maintain and safeguard the **U.S. constitution, abide by federal law, the United Nations Charter, and the Vienna Conventions** through unjustifiable siege against Syria and Iraq and a continued military presence against the sovereign will of the Iraqi Republic and Syrian Arab Republic. These actions, among others, violate the cause of law and justice of nations in addition to the constitution of his own government in complete disregard for the rights of all people.[228] Joseph Robinette Biden Jr. thus warrants an indictment just as prior presidents require prosecution. Professor Richard Falk cited the Nuremberg Trials as enforceable in US courts; that war crimes need judicial restraint by domestic courts.[229] Furthermore, *Bivens* allows for citizens who suffer unconstitutional infringements against their rights

---

[228] *Judicial review grants courts the power to invalidate unconstitutional governmental conduct*

[229] *"Thus the integrity of the nation is staked on those principles (Nuremberg) and today the question is how they apply to our conduct of the war in Vietnam and whether the Unites States Government is prepared to face the consequences of their actions" Taylor, T. (1970). Nuremberg and Vietnam: An American Tragedy. United States: Quadrangle Books.*

to seek redress directly against federal employees guilty of such violations.[230]

Figure 5: Iraqi tribute to Abdel Rahman al-Awlaki in persistent disruptions of McRaven until his fearful resignation

The pursuit of relief through the US federal court system rather than courts whose jurisdiction the United

---

[230] *Bivens v. Six Unknown Named Agents of Fed. Bureau of Narcotics*, **403 U.S. 388, 91 S. Ct. 1999, 29 L. Ed. 2d 619 (1971)**

Senan Shaibani

States refuses to recognize has precedence.[231] [232] Oppressed nationalities within the US achieved partial reparations through arduous struggle thus far but the imperialist state has yet to compensate Arabs and Muslims in any capacity as the effort to colonize Greater Syria continues.[233] The case to indict representatives of the US federal government for crimes against Iraq and Syria fulfill all four requirements necessary to file an action in a federal court.[234] 1) The standing of claimants by virtue of their redressable injury-in-fact caused by unconstitutional government misconduct.[235] [236] 2) The US has violated a

[231] *The TLINGIT AND HAIDA INDIANS OF ALASKA and Harry Douglas et al., Intervenors, v. The UNITED STATES. 389 F.2d 778 (1968)*

[232] *Hersher, R. (2016, September 27). U.S. government to pay $492 million to 17 American Indian tribes. NPR. https://www.npr.org/sections/thetwo-way/2016/09/27/495627997/u-s-government-to-pay-492-million-to-17- american-indian-tribes*

[233] *Allen J Davis, Reparations in the United States - LibGuides at University of Massachusetts Amherst,*

[234] *Supreme Court Rules The Military Commission Act of 2006 Unconstitutional*

[235] *Friends of the Earth, Inc. v. Laidlaw Environmental Services, Inc., 528 U.S. 167 (2000)*

[236] *Massachusetts v. Environmental Protection Agency, 549 U.S. 497 (2007)*

number of laws, foreign and domestic, the enforcement of which has inflicted injuries and concrete material conditions that make the case ripe. 3) The controversy continues without resolution as long as Iraq and Syria remain occupied.[237] 4) The political doctrine fails to apply towards constitutional and federal judiciary questions matters that encroach upon congressional and executive authority simply due to their political overtones relevant to multiple branches of governance.[238] [239] All matters in society and the courts themselves possess a political nature especially legal infractions with political implications that demand prosecution.

"Federal courts are capable of reviewing military decisions, particularly when those decisions cause injury to civilians" and "Damage actions are particularly judicially manageable."[240]

---

[237] *DeFunis v. Odegaard, 416 U.S. 312 (1974)*

[238] *Baker v. Carr, 369 U.S. 186, 278 (1962).*

[239] *Zivotofsky v. Clinton*, **566 U.S. 189 (2012)** *Israeli settlers who disputed the birthplace of their baby as "Israeli" not considered political question and was judiciable*

[240] *Bixby v KBR Inc*, **748 F. Supp. 2d 1224 (D. Or. 2010)**

…

"In addition, because the plaintiffs seek only damages, the granting of relief will not draw the federal courts into conflict with the executive branch. Damage actions are particularly nonintrusive." and "For example, while federal courts are restrained from enjoining on-going state criminal proceedings"[241] there is no such restraint on federal damage actions arising from state criminal proceedings.

…

As the Supreme Court has noted, "historically, damages have been regarded as the ordinary remedy for an invasion of personal interests in liberty".[242]

…

"Numerous district courts have likewise found the political question doctrine inapplicable to tort actions brought against government contractors in the military context"

…

---

[241] *Younger v. Harris*, **401 U.S. 37, 27 L. Ed. 2d 669, 91 S. Ct. 746 (1971),**

[242] *Giulini v. Blessing*, **654 F.2d 189, 193 (2d Cir. 1981).**

The Fifth Circuit has likewise found the political question doctrine inapplicable to tort actions brought against government contractors providing services in support of the Unites States military. On consolidated appeal from three district court decisions that the political question doctrine deprived the court of jurisdiction to consider claims arising out of injuries suffered in Iraq"

The Federal Tort Act of 1946 waives sovereign immunity from cases that arise against misconduct of US government officials even if the injured party accounts only for private individuals rather than entire nation-states. [243] [244] History has established precedence to indict representatives of the US federal government

---

[243] *U.S. Const. 11th Amendment*

[244] *See Limone v. United States,* **579 F.3d 79, 83–84, 102, 108 (1st Cir. 2009)***. See also Bravo v. United States,* **583 F.3d 1297, 1299 n.2 (11th Cir. 2009) (Carnes, J., concurring in the denial of rehearing en banc) (opining that "[t]he facts in the Limone case grew out of one of the darkest chapters in the history of the FBI, which involved rampant misconduct and corruption in the Boston office spanning a period of at least two decades").**

for illegal activities that resemble the domestic "war on terror" abuses.[245] The prosecution of Louis Patrick Gray III who was nominated as director of the FBI, Edward Samuel Miller the deputy assistant director of the inspections division, and Mark Felt special agent who rose to the position of associate director, ultimately led to the indictment of these government employees for civil rights violations, break ins, destruction of evidence, and conspiracy of injuring and oppressing the citizens of the United States.[246] Therefore the legal foundation to counteract the repressive tactics that Arabs and Muslims face today was established in the decolonial era even within American courts. However, what we witness take place entails the inversion of justice where the guilty govern whiles the innocent imprisoned. Restriction of visitations, the denial of mail, the physical obstruction of prayers, the disproportionality in access to food other

---

[245] *Socialist Workers Party v. Attorney Gen. of U.S.*, **642 F. Supp. 1357 (S.D.N.Y. 1986)**

[246] *Clark v. USA*

than pork, excessive bail and fines imposed on Muslims all clearly violates our human and civil rights.[247] [248] [249]

Criminal blockades that prevent Muslims in America the right to pay an obligatory religious tax to Ayatollah Khamenei adds to the injury of the Iraqi and Syrian Republics. The US federal court loses legitimacy if it rejects valid claims made under the federal statute of the Religious Freedom Restoration Act (RFRA) of 1993. In response to narrow interpretations of First Amendment protections, in 1993 Congress passed the Religious Freedom Restoration Act (RFRA), the purpose of which was to restore the principle that the government cannot substantially burden free exercise of religion. Under the RFRA, plaintiffs may obtain injunctive relief or monetary damages against federal officials if they can show that: (1) the government action burdened a sincerely held religious

---

[247] *Iqbal v. Ashcroft,* **574 F.3d 820 (2d Cir. 2009) "terrorists don't have the right to pray"**

[248] *Iran journalist arrested in us, offered to eat pork: Report, News18 (2019), https://www.news18.com/news/world/iran- journalist-arrested-in-us-offered-to-eat-pork-report-2004419.html (last visited Nov 19, 2019).*

[249] *First hand experience when imprisoned for civil disobedience*

belief and (2) that substantial nature of the burden. The paying of one fifth of an income for the underprivileged[250] sincerely reflects religious belief and criminal blockades with a penalty of up to a million dollars and twenty years of jail time without a doubt impose a substantial burden. Although criminal sieges on the right of Muslims to pay religious tax likely violate numerous constitutional rights, claims under the federal statute the Religious Freedom Restoration Act (RFRA) of 1993 stand more likely to succeed than constitutional claims due unfavorable case law.[251] However, the crimes against Iraq and Syria account for such extreme and universally outrageous immoral acts such that their prosecution needs no precedent. In any potential civil rights case against government officials:

> *"People employed by a government agency,*
> *including prison officials, have no higher*
> *station in the community than other persons,*

---

[250] *Know that whatever of a thing you acquire, **a fifth** of it is for Allah, for the Messenger, for the near relative, and the orphans and the needy and they way farer (Qur'an 8:41)*

[251] *See, e.g., KindHearts for Charitable Humanitarian Dev., Inc. v. Geithner,* 647 F. Supp. 2d 857, 888 (N.D. Ohio 2009)

and their testimony is not entitled to any greater weight. All persons stand as equals before the law and are to be dealt with as equals in the court of justice. A prison official who takes the witness stand subjects his testimony to the same examination and the same tests as any other witness and you should not believe an official merely because he or she occupies a high position in the government."[252]

US officials therefore cannot plead sovereign immunity to civil rights cases filed against them. No legitimate trial will regard accusations made by US officials as fact yet dismiss information from the injured parties as mere "allegations" instead of facts.[253]

The settler colonial state wages illegal wars against nations in the name of human rights and a democratic legal system systematically denied to most people domestically

---

[252] *Kerry v. City of Chicago,* **424 F.2d 1134 (7ᵗʰ Cir. 1970)**

[253] *Marion Prisoners' Rights Project. Response to Report and Recommendations of Breed and Ward Report to the Judiciary Committee on Marion Federal Prison (1985). People's Law Office.*

and internationally. **Amnesty International deems that the confinement and treatment of prisoners for their political believes as "cruel, inhuman and degrading"** (*Article 5 of the Universal Declaration of Human Rights*)[254].

International treaties, conventions, minimum standards, rules, declarations and principles violated:

- Basic Principles for the Treatment of Prisoners
- Body of Principles for the Protection of All Persons under Any Form of Detention or Imprisonment
- Declaration on the Elimination of Violence Against Women
- Declaration on the Protection of All Persons from Being Subjected to Torture and Other Cruel, Inhuman or Degrading Treatment of Prisoners

---

[254] *United Nations, 1948, art. 5*

- Principles of medical ethics relevant to the role of health personnel, particularly physicians, in the protection of prisoners and detainees against torture and other cruel, inhuman or degrading treatment or punishment
- Standard Minimum Rules for the Treatment of Prisoners
- Safeguards guaranteeing protection of the rights of those facing the death penalty
- United Nations Rules for the Protection of Juveniles Deprived of their Liberty
- United Nations Standard Minimum Rules for the Administration of Juvenile Justice

The U.S. invasion disregarded these standards in numerous ways like when their supposed medics took Iraqis injured for treatment who then disappeared with their families denied any information by U.S. forces who kidnapped them.[255]

"Political Prisoner": A person incarcerated for actions conducted in assistance of legitimate causes for

---

[255] *Family Relative Shahid Qasim Sayyed Abdel Amir*

self-determination or against the unlawful schemes of the U.S. political establishment.

"Prisoner of War": refers to those combatants struggling against colonial domination and racist regimes captured as prisoners whose treatment requires accordance with the provisions of the **Geneva Conventions Relative to the Treatment of Prisoners of War, of 12 August 1949.**[256] *(General Assembly Resolution 3103 (XXVIII))*. Under the provisions of this treaty, prisoners of war must always receive humane treatment that respects their dignity. It prohibits any unlawful act or omission by the Detention Power which causes death or seriously endangers the health of a prisoner of war in custody as a serious breach of this Convention. Article 3 expressly prohibits "murder of all kinds, mutilation, cruel treatment and torture."

Today Guantanamo Bay violates clearly international law in various ways that include the coercive movement of Muslim political prisoners into a separate country for

---

[256] *International Committee of the Red Cross (ICRC), Geneva Convention Relative to the Treatment of Prisoners of War (Third Geneva Convention), 12 August 1949, 75 UNTS 135*

torture. On March 3, 1989, the UN General Assembly put into effect resolution 43/173 "Body of principles for the protection of all persons under any form of detention or imprisonment" specifically principle 20 which states "if a detained or imprisoned person so requests, he shall if possible be kept in a place of detention or imprisonment reasonable near his usual place of residence".

Filartiga v. Pena-Irala 630 F. 2d 876 (2d Cir. 1980)[257] established by precedent the criminalization of torture as a fundamental principle for international law within the jurisdiction of federal courts that possess the authority to try individuals who violate the universally accepted norms of international and human rights enforceable in the courts of the United States. International law and norms assert that the treatment of prisoners of war "**should be in accordance with the Geneva Convention**"[258] *(Resolution 3103 (XXVIII), 12 December 1973).* Yet **Human Rights Watch** was denied all requests to visit ten major detention facilities across Iraq among which includes the notorious Abu Ghraib

---

[257] *Filartiga v. Pena-Irala, 630 F.2d 876 (2d Cir. 1980)*

[258] *6. U.S.T. 3316.*

and Camp Bucca prisons in addition to more than a dozen internment camps in southern Iraq where innocent Iraqi people that included minors suffered torture, sexual assault, degradation, and unspoken inhuman treatment[259] in violation of *Article 1 of U.N. Resolution 3452 (XXX)[260]*, and the *Declaration on Protection from Torture, 1975.*[261] **Amnesty International** expressed condemnation of "numerous human rights violations against Iraqi juveniles, that include detentions, torture and ill treatment, and killings".

Sundiata Acoli, a political prisoner of war whose a member of the Black Panther Party, wrote that "Abu Ghraib was not an aberration", but rather routine practice of U.S. colonialism reminiscent of the Attica prison. The

---

[259] *Iraq: Hundreds Detained in Degrading Conditions, HUMAN RIGHTS WATCH, (March 13, 2017) https://www.hrw.org/news/2017/03/14/iraq-hundreds-detained-degrading-conditions.*

[260] *UN General Assembly, Declaration on the Protection of All Persons from Being Subjected to Torture and Other Cruel, Inhuman or Degrading Treatment or Punishment, 9 December 1975, A/RES/3452(XXX)*

[261] *UN General Assembly, Declaration on the Protection of All Persons from Being Subjected to Torture and Other Cruel, Inhuman or Degrading Treatment or Punishment, 9 December 1975, A/RES/3452(XXX)*

outrageous crimes in Abu Ghraib resemble the failed attempt to inflict psychological defeat amongst the Vietnamese people through the tiger cages at Con Son, the expansion of the range of techniques of degradation in Afghanistan, torture throughout Latin America that lynched countless Mexicans in their occupied homeland, the reprehensible treatment of Africans who continue to suffer dehumanization centuries later in the American prison industrial complex that illegally rounded up at least 1,200 Muslims without charges indefinitely in the wake of 9/11. The US supreme court held that the "indeterminate detention of [an alien] in a maximum security federal prison under conditions providing less freedom than that granted to ordinary inmates constitutes arbitrary detention and is a violation of customary international law" in ***Rodriguez-Fernandez* (1981)**[262]. The treatment of political prisoners and prisoners of war constitutes torture, cruel, and inhuman treatment that violates *Article 6 of the Universal Declaration of Human Rights*[263] and contravenes most of the *United Nations Standard*

---

[262] *U.S. v. Rodriguez-Fernandez*, **234 F.3d 498 (11th Cir. 2000)**

[263] *United Nations, 1948, art. 6*

Minimum Rules for the Treatment of Prisoners.[264] Today Syrian and Iraqi women and children make up many of the detainees at the Al-Houl Camp[265] controlled by the US occupation that killed over 100 of them this past year alone in violation of *Article 1 of the UN Charter.*[266] Even more egregious conditions exist in the Rukban Camp which has not received any coverage in the Western media despite the severe human rights abuses inflicted against dispossessed Syrian civilians by the US occupation in conjunction with their sectarian militias at the illegal base.[267]

To the contrary, The Syrian Arab Republic passed an anti-torture law to criminalize physical abuse of

---

[264] [266]*UN General Assembly, United Nations Standard Minimum Rules for the Treatment of Prisoners (the Nelson Mandela)*

[265] *See Devorah Margolin, Detention Facilities in Syria, Iraq Remain Vulnerable to Islamic State Attacks, WASHINGTON INSTITUTE, (Sept. 29, 2022) https://www.washingtoninstitute.org/policy-analysis/detention-facilities-syria-iraq-remain- vulnerable-islamic-state-attacks.*

[266] *United Nations, Charter of the United Nations, 24 October 1945, 1 UNTS XVI*

[267] *Noor Ibrahim, Stay and Starve, or Leave and Die, FOREIGN POLICY, (Oct. 26, 2020) https://foreignpolicy.com/2020/10/26/al-tanf-rukban-refugee-syria-humanitarian/.*

prisoners.[268] One Syrian man who requested his name remain anonymous was released from the prison branch 227 after President Assad issued an amnesty for deserters from the Syrian Arab Army. He spoke of how the physicians, health care workers, and even military generals took measures to ensure acceptable standards for the imprisoned with regular checkups to inquire if anyone was mistreated, inadequately fed, or ill and required medical attention as international law requires.[269] While the US backed FSA that called for genocide of entire segments of the Syrian population turned a school in a Damascus district comprised of underprivileged Alawis into a prison. Where kidnapped Syrians endured torture as mercenaries held them for ransoms as one of many war crimes committed with US complicity that promoted a false narrative that Alawites control Syria to justify their mass executions. A Syrian soldier from that underprivileged community where a school was

---

[268] *Manar Salameh, President al-Assad issues law that incriminates torture Syrian Arab News Agency (2022), https://www.sana.sy/en/?p=268111 (last visited Nov 21, 2022).*

[269] *Syria's Assad issues yet another amnesty for draft dodgers, 2022 WLNR 41696092*

transformed into a concentration camp was arrested by Syrian authorities for an accident that killed a driver who sped towards his checkpoint in a volatile war zone. Even though the Sunni family pardoned the Alawi Solder (most Syrian soldiers belong to Sunni Islam and refrain from "Alawi" or "Sunni" descriptions promoted by imperialism) who both live under the poverty line he still faces jail time. Contrast this with reports of American soldiers who murdered entire Iraqi families that drove towards checkpoints with the encouragement of their generals. Regular Alawis in Syria in no way benefit uniquely from Pan Arab rule and hold no privileges. Palestinian fighters on the side of the Syrian Arab Republic told me in Damascus that the Syrian government grants them far more privileges than Syrian Alawis to emphasize the real nature of the war on Syria as the main supporter of resistance organizations in Palestine & Lebanon. Dr. Abdul-Aziz Al- Khair the longest held political prisoner in Syria belongs to the Alawi minority. Which adds to the refutation of the false narrative to scapegoat an oppressed minority for the economic and political problems suffered by Syrians collectively.

Figure 6: 'Ish al Wer-wer Slum

War Crimes & Genocide

The General Assembly Resolution 260 (A) (II) of the United States Convention on War Crimes and Crimes Against Humanity, Including Genocide (December 9, 1948)[272] reads as follows: Article II:

In the present Convention, genocide means any of the following acts committed with **the intent to destroy, in whole or in part, a national, ethnical, racial, or religious group as such:**

1. **Killing members of the group;**
2. **Causing serious bodily or mental harm to members of the group;**
3. **Deliberately inflicting on the group conditions of life calculated to bring about its physical destruction in whole or in part;**

4. **Imposing measures intended to prevent births within the group;**

5. **Forcibly transferring children of the group to another group.**[270]

Representatives of the US regime committed war crimes outlined in Article II of Control Council Law No. 10.[271] Which reads:

> "Atrocities or offences against persons or property, constituting violations of the laws or customs of war, including but not limited to, murder, ill treatment or deportation to slave labour or for any other purpose of civilian population from occupied territory, murder or ill treatment of prisoners of war or persons on the seas, killing of hostages, plunder of public or private property, wanton destruction of

---

[270] *78 U.N.T.S. 277.*

[271] *Executive Order 9858, May 31, 1947, 12 Fed.Reg. 3555*

cities, towns or villages, or devastation not justified by military necessity."[272]

US led wars against Iraq and Syria constitute a policy of genocide that killed, injured, widowed, and orphaned the lives of millions from both nations. Endless violations against Iraq and now Syria continue with impunity that caused one of the greatest diasporas in the world. The US has targeted autonomous states such as Iraq and Syria that rejected neo-colonialism in attempt to transform them into a captive market and cheap source of raw materials in a strategic region.[273] Among the consequences of U.S. led efforts to liquidate the national identities of Iraq and Syria has unfolded in the mass dispersal of millions of Syrians and Iraqis into the urban centers of colonialism for the exploitation of their labor. The "international refugee crisis" was caused by the genocidal campaigns of Western

---

[272] *Control Council Law No. 10, Punishment of persons Guilty of War Crimes, Crimes Against Peace and Against Humanity, Dec. 20, 1945, 3 OFFICIAL GAZETTE CONTROL COUNCIL FOR GERMANY 50–55 (1946).*

[273] *Trump Keeps Talking About 'keeping' Middle East oil. That would be illegal. James G. Stewart. 2020. "There's a well established international standard outlawing "pillage".*

imperialism that exploited the forced migration to the benefit of neo colonialism rather than the national welfare of the Iraqi and Syrian people.[274] The occupation of Iraq and Syria, the devastation to their national economy, forced migration with false promises of rewards to those who collaborated with U.S. forces against the resistance movements, the most recent diaspora in the U.S. made up of lower classes of society to serve as a permanent source of cheap labor for North American capital, all make apparent the genocide inflicted against Iraq and Syria.

The U.S., which masquerades itself as a world-leader in human rights and justice, has tried to place itself above international law throughout the entirety of American history (whether treaties with Native Nations or international law). U.S. aggression against Iraq and Syria raises the international criminality of U.S. government officials. **Article 5 of the Statute of the International Criminal Court (37 I.L.M. 999):**

---

[274] *T.J. Petrowski, The refugee crisis is a crisis of imperialism CounterPunch.org (2015), https://www.counterpunch. org/2015/09/11/the-refugee-crisis-is-a-crisis-of-imperialism/ (last visited Oct 2, 2015).*

"Although classical aggression has generally been thought to involve direct military operations by regular national forces under government control, today subjugation and control of peoples may well result from resort to non-military methods. Economic pressures on the other states; demands couched in traditional diplomatic terms but laden with implied threats to compel action or inaction; fifth column activities; the endless propaganda harangue urging another state's peoples to rise against their government; the aiding and abetting of rebel bands intent on overthrowing another government; and a wide range of other modern techniques must be included in the concept of aggression in so far as they are delicts at international law, for they are directed against the sovereign independence of a state." Ann Van Wynen Thomas & A.J. Thomas Jr., *The Concept of Aggression in International Law* (1972).[275]

More than any other form of criminality, Wars of Aggression inflict destruction upon human life, civilizations, and history. For that reason, **the Nuremberg**

---

[275] *Ann Van Wynen Thomas & A.J. Thomas Jr., The Concept of Aggression in International Law (1972).*

Senan Shaibani

Tribunal proclaimed wars of aggression as "the supreme international crime."[276] While government officials in Africa frequently face trials before the International Criminal Court, none of the high-ranked U.S. regime officials faced justice for incomparable war crimes they commit such as that in Iraq or Syria. It remains provable beyond doubt the illegality of decades of US aggression against Iraq and Syria through several legal arguments that build the case to hold the US officials accountable for violations of international law in Iraq and Syria.

The Charter of the UN denies signatory states from any unilateral action towards the use of force in cases where imminent, certain, and immediate threat of the use of force remains absent. This obligation exists under **Art 2 (4) of the UN Charter**:

> **"All members shall refrain in their international relations from the threat or use of force against the territorial integrity or political independence of any state, or [behave] in any other**

---

[276] *82 U.N.T.S. 279.*

118

**manner inconsistent with the purposes
of the United Nations."**[277]

In the contemplation of the Iraqi invasion, the U.S. attempted to create false legal justifications to excuse war against Iraq and later Syria using self-defense under UN Charter **Article 51 (regarding self- defense), Chapter VII (which concerns collective action), and humanitarian intervention.** All three justifications hold neither factual nor legal basis under international law.

The U.S. adopted multiple underlying arguments to justify the war against Iraq as follows:

1) **The U.S. argued a connection between the attack in 9/11 and Iraq, specifically the Baathist government, which later proved false as admitted by the Bush regime.**

According to Richard Clarke – the National Coordinator for Security, Infrastructure Protection, and "Counterterrorism" in the Bush regime – key foreign policy planners maneuvered to take advantage of the

---

[277] *U.N. Charter art. 2, 4.*

tragedy to carry out a previously planned policy to invade Iraq.[278] <u>President Bush was personally</u> advised by Clarke that al Qaeda committed the attacks and that Iraq had no connection with Al-Qaeda.[279]

Leaders in the administration disregarded this evidence and insisted on false claims that a connection between Iraq and the September 11 attacks exists as a pillar of the prewar effort to rally public support for an invasion of Iraq.[280] After the invasion, <u>President Bush and Secretary Powell stated they lacked any proof that connects Saddam Hussein to al Qaeda,[281] which rules out the possibility of an Article 51 exemption based on no Iraqi involvement in the September 11 attacks.</u> Furthermore,

---

[278] *See Bruce Riedel, 9/11 and Iraq: The making of a tragedy, BROOKINGS, (Sept. 17, 2021) https://www.brookings.edu/blog/order-from-chaos/2021/09/17/9-11-and-iraq-the-making-of-a-tragedy/.*

[279] *Richard A. Clarke, Five Inauguration Days: The US and the Middle East, 71 THE MIDDLE EAST JOURNAL 147, 148 (2017).*

[280] *Supra note 205, Riedel.*

[281] *Christopher Marquis, THE SSTRUGGLE FOR IRAQ: DIPLOMACY; Powell Admits No Hard Proof Linking Iraw to Al Qaeda, N.Y. TIMES, (Jan. 9, 2004) https://www.nytimes.com/2004/01/09/world/struggle-for-iraq-diplomacy-powell-admits- no-hard-proof-linking-iraq-al-qaeda.html.*

the delinquent American president Bush stated that "even if regime change happens, the American army will still invade Iraq." U.S. bullets funded by U.S. taxes murdered journalists in Iraq in violation of **Protocol 1 Article 4(A)(4)** of the **Third Geneva Convention. Article 79**[282] establishes that members of the press in dangerous areas of hostilities count as civilians within the definition of **Article 50(1)**. Therefore, international humanitarian law affords them complete protection as civilians. One of the many blatant violations of this established norm took place in the Palestine Hotel in Baghdad where American airstrikes unlawfully murdered at least three journalists and wounded many more in April of 2003.[283] **Moreover, the US argued the existence of nuclear and chemical**

---

[282] *International Committee of the Red Cross (ICRC), Geneva Convention Relative to the Treatment of Prisoners of War (Third Geneva Convention), 12 August 1949, 75 UNTS 135*

[283] *Rockets Hit Hotel in Baghdad; Shiite Rebel Offers Truce Deal, REUTERS, (Oct. 7, 2004) https://www.nytimes.com/2004/10/07/ international/middleeast/rockets-hit-hotel-in-baghdad-shiite-rebel-offers- 2004100793880512349.html.*

weapons in Iraq, and thus the need for self-defense under Art. 51 of the UN Charter.[284]

Again, that argument proved factually and legally flawed. In fact, between 1991 and 1998, Iraq was subject to inspections by the United Nations Special Commission (UNSCOM), which confirmed that the country had destroyed all biological and chemical weapons it received from the United States in the first place as well as any nuclear weapons program.[285] Hussein Kamel, a former Iraqi official who managed the national weapons programs, said that the country had destroyed all arsenals of Iraqi weapons and the missiles used to launch them. Up until the time of the invasion, the International Atomic Energy Agency (IAEA), led by Mohammed ElBaradei, and the UN Monitoring, Verification, and Inspection Commission (UNMOVIC), headed by Hans Blix, both

---

[284] *United Nations, Charter of the United Nations, 24 October 1945, 1 UNTS XVI*

[285] *IRAQ: Weapons Inspections: 1991-1998, COUNCIL ON FOREIGN RELATIONS, (Feb. 3, 2005) https://www.cfr.org/backgrounder/iraq-weapons-inspections-1991-1998.*

conducted operations in Iraq.[286] They reported that they failed to locate either operational weapons of mass destruction or any facilities to create them.[287]

No proof exists of any chemical, biological, or nuclear weapons in Iraq before or after the U.S. invasion in 2003.[288] The Syrian government joined the **Chemical Weapons Convention** from the start of the imposed war and continues to submit monthly reports to **Director-General of the Organization for the Prohibition of Chemical Weapons** that prove the absence of such weapons and facilities.[289] Even if such weapons existed, they fail to constitute self-defense under **Article 51 of the UN Charter**, which demands an imminent and certain threat of the use of force or its use.[290] Mere anticipatory or preventive self-defense has no justification under **Art.**

---

[286] *Richard Sanders, What Did Happen to Saddam's WMD?, HISTORY TODAY, (July 12, 2016) https://www.historytoday.com/what-did-happen-saddam's-wmd.*

[287] *Supra note 210, Sanders.*

[288] *IRAQ: Weapons Inspections: 1991-1998, COUNCIL ON FOREIGN RELATIONS, (Feb. 3, 2005) https://www.cfr.org/backgrounder/iraq-weapons-inspections-1991-1998.*

[289] *1974 U.N.T.S. 45.*

[290] *U.N. Charter art. 51.*

51 of the UN Charter as self-defense.[291] Although such weapons never existed in Iraq before, during, and after the U.S. occupation according to mentioned UN reports, the mere possession of such weapons will not allow the threat of the use of force that triggers self-defense under international law. Current international law, as noted by M. Ratner (a leading international law scholar), stipulates that the use of armed force and the invasion of another territory of a state only has justification if in self-defense when: **1. An armed attack is launched or immediately threatened; 2. Defensive action against that attack is urgently required; 3. There is no real alternative for measures in self- defense; and 4. The act in self-defense limits itself to the need to end or avert the attack.**[292]

All these conditions never existed in both the Iraqi and Syrian cases. As such, the US has no valid self-defense

---

[291] *Id.*

[292] *Steven R. Ratner, "Self-Defense Against Terrorists: The Meaning of Armed Attack." In Counter-terrorism Strategies in a Fragmented International Legal Order: Meeting the Challenges, edited by N. Schrijver and L. van den Herik, 334-55 (2013).*

justification under **Article 51 of the UN Charter.**[293] The use of force unjustly to protect an unjust political agenda against Iraq and Syria constitutes a supreme international crime that justifies Iraqi and Syrian self-defense against U.S. imperialism that necessitates accountability on a worldwide scale.

2) **Further, the US argued "humanitarian intervention" to preserve the human rights of Iraqi and Syrian people against the Baathist government:**

The economic blockade imposed on Iraq from 1990 to 2003 constitutes one of the worst humanitarian catastrophes committed in the name of globalism. This siege violated the **Protocol 1 of the Geneva Conventions**[294] as they "cause incidental loss of civilian life, injury to civilians... or a combination thereof" more than concrete and direct military advantage anticipated. At least half a million Iraqi children lost their lives due to

---

[293] *United Nations, Charter of the United Nations, 24 October 1945, 1 UNTS XVI*

[294] *1125 U.NN.T.S. 3.*

the blockade which amounts to human rights violations followed by the illegal military occupation in 2003.[295] Based on false claims, Western imperialists, particularly the U.S. and UK, fervently supported illegal besiegement at the cost of countless innocent lives as a form of collective punishment to topple the non-compliant Iraqi authorities. The Geneva International Centre for Justice (GICJ) was dismayed at the crimes committed against the Iraqi civilian population under the siege.[296] The consequences of and subsequent acts of aggression against innocent people continue in the ravaged country with devastation. The Syrian Arab Republic face increased restrictions that apply to business anywhere that engage the Syrian political establishment or sections of the Syrian economy.[297] Even when those business relations lack any relation to the

---

[295] *Barbara Crossette, Iraq Sanctions Kill Children, U.N. Reports, N.Y. TIMES, (Dec. 1, 1995) https://www.nytimes.com/1995/12/01/world/iraq-sanctions-kill-children-un-reports.html.*

[296] *Razing the Truth About Sanctions Against Iraq, GENEVA INTERNATIONAL CENTRE FOR JUSTICE, (last visited Jan. 11, 2023) https://www.gicj.org/positions-opinons/gicj-positions-and-opinions/1188-razing-the-truth-about-sanctions-against-iraq.*

[297] *Syria Sanctions, U.S. DEPARTMENT OF STATE, (last visited Jan. 11, 2023) https://www.state.gov/syria-sanctions/.*

U.S. regime. The material conditions of Syria prior to the war demonstrate the nature of modern imperialism as an international system and the way it acts within non-compliant states amid peace when the American government has yet to carry out attacks that follow the inability to attain objectives for profits irrespective of the repercussions. The Caesar Act against the Syrian Arab Republic indefensibly violates human rights of housing, heath, and the standard of life and development.[298] UN experts call for an immediate end to the unilateral siege on Syria.[299] **The UN General Assembly and the Human Rights Council repudiated the blockade as illegal.**[300]

---

[298] *H.R. 31, 116th Cong. (2019).*

[299] *UN envoy Geir Pedersen said that U.S. sanctions on Syria shouldn't block humanitarian assistance December 7, 2022*

[300] *Rebecca Barber, The New U.S. "Ceasar" Sanctions on Syria Are Illegal, JUST SECURITY, (July 8, 2020) https://www.justsecurity. org/71189/the-new-u-s-caesar-sanctions-on-syria-are-illegal/ ; see High Commissioner to Human Rights Council: Sanctions Can Create Severe and Undue Suffering for Individuals who have Neither Perpetrated Crimes nor Otherwise Borne Responsibility for Improper Conduct, UNITED NATIONS HUMAN RIGHTS OFFICE OF THE HIGH COMMISSIONER, (Sept. 16, 2021) https://www. ohchr.org/en/press-releases/2021/09/high-commissioner-human-rights-council-sanctions-can- create-severe-and-undue.*

In the most recent resolution on the subject, the General Assembly said that it "strongly object[ed]" to international embargo, and "call[ed] upon all member states neither to recognize those measures nor to apply them." Genocidal sieges that produce widespread poverty heightened by the Caesar Act amid a global pandemic raise serious concerns under international law. The U.S. regime abruptly imposes trade embargoes on oppressed Arab nations as they try to recover from U.S. backed wars yet condemn boycotts, divestments, and sanctions against the illegal Israeli invasion of the Levant.

Corporate greed of oil monopolies and arms manufacturers guides US warfare with the objective solely for the profit of a few and never for "humanitarianism". The greatest humanitarian crises on earth right now—from Gaza to Yemen—resulted from "humanitarian" U.S. led intervention that devastated Syria and Iraq in the name of "humanitarianism". The Syrian army tried to negotiate with sectarian factions that invaded Syrian cities, provided humanitarian aid, and allowed any civilians the opportunity to evacuate several times through humanitarian corridors unlike the U.S. assault on Raqqa.[301] The disproportionality in civilian casualties and destruction between the Syrian liberation of Aleppo and the

U.S. invasion of Raqqa vastly contrast.[302] Especially since the Syrian Arab Republic defended its territorial integrity pursuant to Resolution 2165[303] unlike the US invasion of another country. Western imperialism seeks to exploit nations for markets and natural resources, not save lives.

No "humanitarian intervention" justification exists under international law. The principle was invented by the Bush regime to invade Iraq and it has never become a state practice as a part of customary international law, let alone a part of any international treaty. In contrast, UN member states widely rejected it because the permission of the use

---

[301] *Aleppo Was Not Broken in Darkness. Eva Bartlett. JSTOR*

[302] *Net, Al Mayadeen. "Syria: Time Has Come to Shed Light on US Coalition Crimes in Raqqa." Al Mayadeen English, 18 Apr. 2022, https://english.almayadeen.net/news/politics/syria:-time-has-come-to-shed-light-on-us-coalition-crimes-in.*

[303] *UN Security Council, Security Council resolution 2165 (2014) [on the humanitarian situation in the Syrian Arab Republic and the establishment of a monitoring mechanism], 14 July 2014, S/RES/2165(2014)*

of force to protect people against their governments upon a "humanitarian intervention" argument will evolve as a tool for imperialism and colonialism.

Normand – another leading international law scholar – opines that "the legally dubious doctrine of humanitarian intervention, emerged as a new concept that has not gained the support of the international law community."

A clear example of apathy for the welfare of the Iraqi people by their so called liberators includes the disregard for the consequences of the complete blockade imposed on Iraq in the aftermath of two consecutive wars that took over a million lives.. According to UNICEF estimates, these subsequent restrictions, supported by both republican and democratic administrations, resulted in the deaths of up to over one million more Iraqis.[304] Excluded from these numbers include other civilians who also died from sporadic American strikes against Iraq between the end of the Gulf War in 1991 and the beginning of the Iraq war in 2003. Over a decade before the US employed chemical weapons against Fallujah, an American missile

---

[304] *Supra note 220, Razing the Truth About Sanctions Against Iraq.*

massacred one hundred and thirty unarmed civilians.[305] Another attack on a bridge in Nasriyah took the lives of forty-seven innocent civilians.[306] Witnesses among Iraqi residents testified that civilians comprised the target of US airstrikes against the highway that leads west to Jordan from Iraq in 1991.

Among the violations of the Geneva Convention in this period includes attacks against medical vehicles that clearly indicated themselves as part of the United Nations, Red Crescent, and Red Cross. The Pentagon never denied that the U.S. struck civilian targets such as another bus they struck that burned thirty to forty people to death. On February 13, 1991 near the time of dawn prayers U.S. forces launched an assault on the Amariyah shelter that killed 408 Iraqi civilians.[307] Among the first targets of

---

[305] *Off Target: The Conduct of the War and Civilian Casualties in Iraq, HUMAN RIGHTS WATCH, (Dec. 11, 2003) https://www.hrw.org/report/2003/12/11/target/conduct-war-and-civilian-casualties-iraq.*

[306] *Id.*

[307] *Sofia Barbarani, Amiriyah bombing 30 years on: 'No one remembers' the victims, ALJAZEERA, (Feb. 13, 2021) https://www.aljazeera.com/features/2021/2/13/amiriyah-bombing-30-years-on-no-one-remembers-the-victims.*

cowardly American airstrikes was an infant and baby milk process facility in Baghdad over 400 miles away from Kuwait. An estimated 3,000 infant deaths took place in Iraq within a span of a year due to US imperialism.[308]

> (b) **War Crimes:** Violations of the laws or customs of war which include, but are not limited to, murder, ill- treatment or deportation to slave-labor or for any other purpose of civilian population of or in occupied territory, murder or ill- treatment of prisoners of war, of persons on the seas, killing of hostages, plunder of public or private property, wanton destruction of cities, towns, or villages, or devastation not justified by military necessity.

---

[308] *Roger Dobson, Perinatal mortality in Iraq more than tripled since sanctions, PUBMED CENTRAL, (Mar. 8, 2003) https://www.ncbi. nlm.nih.gov/pmc/articles/PMC1169290/.*

> (c) **Crimes Against Humanity:** Murder, extermination, enslavement, deportation and other inhuman acts done against any civilian population, or persecutions on political, racial or religious grounds, when such acts are done or such persecutions are carried on in execution of or in connection with any crime against peace or any war crime.

In what amounted to the infamous "highway of death", the military command of the United States never made any attempt to differentiate between military members and civilians. This was a form of collective punishment after Iraq broke with Sykes Picot in the move into Kuwait and launched rockets at the Zionist invasion.[309] International law specifically forbids the type of indiscriminate and excessive use of force employed by U.S. forces. American aircraft disabled cars and vehicles from the front and the back of the major road in southern Iraq from Basra into Kuwait to trap civilians as well as convoys of conscripted Iraqi soldiers who

---

[309] *"Unmaking of Arab Socialism" Ali Kadri.*

completely withdrew from Kuwait in accordance with
United Nations Resolution 660.[310] About forty miles of
highway witnessed tens of thousands of Iraqis, Kuwaitis,
and Palestinians burn alive.[311] This mass murder of Arabs
across Iraq despite the Iraqi withdrawal from Kuwait was
followed by air raids against civilian targets that include
mosques and "no fly zones" over Iraqi airspace. Contrast
this with the total U.S. support for the Saudi military
invasion of Yemen and Bahrain in violation of the Leahy
laws[312]. Contrast the obvious contradiction between U.S.
condemnation of Saddam Hussein in Kuwait while it
continues to support the Israeli occupation of the West
Bank, Gaza, and all historic Palestine.

The obvious and swift incineration of their bodies
indicates the use of napalm, phosphorus, and other
banned substances, used later against Fallujah, Mosul,

---

[310] *UN Security Council, Security Council resolution 660 (1990) [Iraq-Kuwait], 2 August 1990, S/RES/660 (1990)*

[311] *Steve Coll, U.S. Scrambled To Shape View Of 'Highway of Death', THE WASHINGTON POST, (March 11, 1991) https://www. washingtonpost.com/archive/politics/1991/03/11/us-scrambled-to-shape-view-of-highway-of-death/05899d9a-f304-441d-8078-59812cdacc5c/.*

[312] *22 U.S.C. § 2378d; 10 U.S.C. § 362.*

and Raqqa, by a coalition led by the United States.[313] *The Geneva Protocols of 1977* forbade their use.[314] *The Geneva Convention of 1949, Common Article 3*, forbids the murder of soldiers "out of combat" like the Iraqi soldiers who left Kuwait. U.S. Ambassador to Iraq in 1991, April Glaspie, deceptively signaled the greenlight to Saddam Hussein that Iraqi action against Kuwait after repeated failed negotiations will not incur any consequences from the American political establishment.[315] Permanent Representative to the UN from Iraq in 1961 when Baghdad first attempted to nationalize the oil industry, Adnan Pachachi, asserted that the British tried to exclude Kuwait from the Iraqi state with the use of the illegal 1899 treaty as their pretext to separate Kuwait from Iraq. In 1938 most of the members of the Legislative Council in Kuwait voted in favor of reunification with Iraq. Nevertheless,

---

[313] *George Monbiot, The US used chemical weapons in Iraq – and then lied about it, THE GUARDIAN, (Nov. 14, 2005) https://www. theguardian.com/politics/2005/nov/15/usa.iraq.*

[314] *1125 U.N.T.S. 3; 1125 U.N.T.S. 609.*

[315] *Stephen M. Walt, WikiLeaks, April Glaspie, and Saddam Hussein, FOREIGN POLICY, (Jan. 9, 2011) https://foreignpolicy. com/2011/01/09/wikileaks-april-glaspie-and-saddam-hussein/.*

the U.S. took the lives of at least 300,000 Iraqi people in the 1991 Gulf War before the 2003 invasion with the outlawed chemical agents.

At the time of invasion in 2003, there was no proof that the Iraqi government induced a humanitarian crisis that resulted in a significant loss of human life, according to Hillary Charlesworth – who serves as a current ICJ judge and a prominent international law scholar. The evidence shows only proof that the U.S. caused a humanitarian catastrophe. Finally, the U.S. intervention in Iraq was a far cry from "humanitarian." It caused far more atrocities, such as over one million Iraqi civilians killed in the occupation, than whatever human breaches the US government claimed to defend against the Iraqi government.

3) **The existence of UN Security Council resolutions No. 678** [316] **and 1441 that falsely justify the invasion of Iraq under Chapter VII of the UN Charter:**

---

[316] *UN Security Council, Security Council resolution 678 (1990) [Iraq-Kuwait], 29 November 1990, S/RES/678 (1990)*

America, Britain, and Spain pursued a Security Council resolution to declare Iraq in violation of weapons deactivation resolutions **(Resolution 1441),** and that this represented a danger to global "security".[317] Such a resolution was never approved by UN security council. Hans Blix – an international law scholar & Former Minister for Foreign Affairs of Sweden – observed that the reluctance of the UN security council to adopt the U.S. draft resolution meant that "the Council dissociated the UN from an armed action that most member states thought was not justified at any rate, not at this stage."

After such failure, the U.S. attempted to interpret **UN Security Council resolutions Nos. 678 and 1441**[318] as a continued invitation for military intervention in Iraq.[319] Yet, neither resolution authorized the use of force on behalf of the United Nations. *UN Resolution No. 1441* – issued in 2002 – strengthened the UN weapons inspection process

---

[317] *S.C. Res. 1441 (2002).*

[318] *UN Security Council, Security Council resolution 1441 (2002) [concerning Iraq], 8 November 2002, S/RES/1441 (2002)*

[319] *S.C. Res. 678 (1990); S.C. Res. 1441 (2002).*

in Iraq by sending a new inspection team (UNMOVIC)[320].
When the U.S. decided to invade Iraq, the UNMOVIC
inspection mechanism was already in existence, that
functioned with the Iraqi reasonable assistance, and was
nearly complete in evaluation as to whether Iraq complied
with the requirements of *UN Resolutions 687 and 1441* –
according to Hans Blix. Again, such resolution, by its
very nature, never authorized any military intervention
in Iraq by any member state, neither the U.S. nor anyone
else.[321] *UN Resolution 687* not only stated that sanctions
against Iraq will end after compliance from Baghdad
with disarmament.[322] The resolution called for a region
free from weapons of mass destruction which effectively
proves the illegality of Israeli nuclear weapons supplied
by the United States.

As such, none of the U.S. legal arguments based on
Art. 51[323], humanitarian intervention, or Chapter VII

---

[320]   *S.C. Res. 1441 (2002).*

[321]   *Krieger, David. "The War on Iraq as Illegal and Illegitimate."*
    Nuclear Age Peace Foundation, 1 July 2013, https://www.
    wagingpeace.org/the-war-on-iraq-as-illegal-and-illegitimate/.

[322]   *S.C. Res. 678 (1990).*

[323]   *U.N. Charter art. 51.*

collective action hold up factually or legally. And thus, the U.S. officials remain culpable for the breach of *Art 2 (4) of the UN Charter* for using military force to invade Iraq in 2003.[324]

Furthermore, the U.S. also remains responsible for the warfare in Syria despite the false pretext of the "war on terror". The costly so called war on terror only perpetuated the very problems it proclaimed to resolve. The "war on terrorism" in Syria represents another fabrication of the "humanitarian intervention" argument that is widely rejected as an **exception to Art. 2 (4) of the UN Charter**, which prohibits the use of force.[325] It was amid the war on Iraq that the first U.S. military attack on Syrian soil took place against a family of eight civilians in 2008. This crime against humanity demonstrates how the Syrian Arab Republic was rendered a target of US aggression for the autonomous support provided to Iraqi Resistance against the US occupation as well as military aid to anti-Zionist forces in the Levant such as Hezbollah and Hamas who effectively liberated land from the Israeli occupation.

---

[324] *U.N. Charter art. 2, 4.*

[325] *U.N. Charter art. 2, 4.*

I. The US war on Iraq and Syria constitutes <u>state</u> <u>crimes</u> under which US officials involved need to face justice.

Representation of the Iraqi & Syria will decide whether to push the UN General Assembly to establish international criminal tribunals to place US officials on trial and the avenues for justice. These efforts will normalize the recognition of US regime criminality and give impetus to civil society and solidarity movements in the struggle against US led imperialism. The Iraqi experience demonstrated, however, the limited capacity of the US judiciary to prosecute US war criminals and the limitations of protests alone. It was under Iraqi jurisdiction that US crimes took place and thus Iraqi forces justifiably detained US military personnel and prosecuted them[326] but the primary culprits still need to face trial. The sovereign will of Syrian and Iraqi parliamentary authorities and members of the diaspora

---

[326] *Anti-War News Articles: Three US Contractors Kidnapped in Baghdad, 2016 WLNR 1599750.* <u>*"US embassy confirmed that Shi'ite Militias kidnapped several American contractors"*</u>

possess standing to file claims against US officials under the jurisdiction of the ICJ, Syria, Iran, or even the US. The basis on which to indict the US federal government exists nationally and internationally which allows for legal action to emerge civilly and criminally in the form of a national, private (arbitral) body, or international court that with the jurisdiction to effectively hold the US government accountable for war crimes and violations of human rights. US government efforts to impose its illegal jurisdiction over Iraq overtly and Syria covertly demands prosecution under an official judiciary with authority to apply justice.

Principle III

The fact that a person who committed an act which constitutes a crime under international law acted as Head of State or responsible Government official does not relieve him from responsibility under international law.

Principle IV

The fact that a person acted pursuant to order of his Government or of a superior does not relieve him from responsibility under international law, provided a moral choice was in fact possible to him.

In 1988, William Chambliss – an American criminologist – defined a **"state crime"** as acts considered criminal under the law perpetrated by state officials in the course of their employment as agents of the state.[327] For example, a member of law enforcement who uses unjustified force against innocent civilians commits a state

---

[327] *Chambliss, W. J. (1988). Exploring Criminology. New York: Macmillan.*

crime. Yet states often face reluctance for accountability before international law. Chambliss later added that state crimes need to encompass an act that transgresses international treaties and standards established in the courts and agreements of international entities.

Because international law was recognized by every country - violations constitute criminal offenses. According to **Article II, section 2 of the US Constitution,** approved treaties, such as the **UN Charter and Geneva Conventions**, received recognition as the ultimate law of the land in America.[328] The Supreme Court in *Asakura v. Seattle,* **256 U.S. 332, 341 (1924)**[329] stated that treaties in US courts necessitate interpretation in a broad spirit. If two constructions possibly exist, with one more restrictive of rights that lay claim under it and the other favorable to them, the latter takes precedence. Furthermore, in *Sullivan v. Kidd,* **254 U.S. 433 (1921)**[330] the Court stated that treaties rely upon the same principles as written contracts between individuals, with all parts understood

---

[328] *U.S. CONST. art. 2, § 2.*

[329] *Asakura v. Seattle,* **256 U.S. 332, 341 (1924)**

[330] *Sullivan v. Kidd,* **254 U.S. 433 (1921)**

in the view of a fair operation to the treaty, and their execution in utmost good faith to effectuate the purposes of the high contractual parties.

The International Law Commission revived an idea of state criminal liability in 1976, realizing that under international law, a tight relationship exists among state criminal responsibility and individual criminal liability. The International Law Commission arrived at the conclusion that:

> " …most of the offences that international criminal law proscribes and for the perpetration of which it endeavors to punish the individuals that allegedly committed them, also are regarded by international law as particularly serious violations by States: They are international delinquencies entailing the "aggravated responsibility" of the State on whose behalf the perpetrators may have acted. Thus, when one of these crimes is committed by an individual not acting

in a private capacity, a dual responsibility may follow: **criminal liability of the individual, falling under international criminal law, and State responsibility, regulated by international rules on this matter.**"

All the crimes committed by the US in Iraq count as state crimes that give rise to the international responsibility of US officials. As provided in the Human Rights Watch Report produced in 2003[331], these state crimes include:

1) **use of cluster bombs against Iraq;**
2) **attempts to "decapitate" key Iraqi officials**
3) **murder of many Iraqis;**
4) **use of napalm, firebombs;**
5) **indiscriminate use of depleted uranium munitions**

---

[331] *Docherty, B. L., & Garlasco, M. E. (2003). Off target: The conduct of the war and civilian casualties in Iraq. Human Rights Watch Ibrahim, A. P. D. I. H. (2022).*

Which emit hazardous chemical waste and causes prolonged environmental concerns that made Iraqi people vulnerable to considerable toxicity. The United Nations considers the depleted uranium ammunition used against Iraq by American forces for decades as illegal "Weapons of Mass Destruction".[332] These atrocities amount to state crimes because the orders to commit those heinous crimes originated from the Bush regime as well as previous and subsequent administrations in their official capacity as agents of the United States.[333] As such, the U.S. regime officials need to all face an international trial for the state crimes committed in Iraq and Syria. Previous and subsequent US administrations, both republican and democrat, also conspired to and committed crimes against humanity in Iraq and Syria. As early as 1958, the CIA pursued a policy to covertly deliver arms that included

---

[332] *Sub-Commission on Prevention of Discrimination and Protection of Minorities. United Nations Human Rights Commission. Depleted Uranium UN Resolutions. Retrieved 16 January 2011.*

[333] *The American Strategy Towards Iraq During The Trump Era And Beyond. Journal of Positive School Psychology; 2095- 2109. Peterson, J. (2007*

napalm so long as it was "convincingly deniable".[334] The United States supplied **chemical weapons and the so called "weapons of mass destruction"** it invaded Iraq under the pretext of decades after they oversaw their use against the Kurdish and Iranian people in the 1980s.

Furthermore, the occupier nation remains obligated to preserve public order in the invaded territory in line with **international law**, **the Geneva Convention**, and the **Convention (IV)**[335] with regards to the Laws and Customs of War on Land. *Therefore, the thousands of suicide attacks and car bombs against the Iraqi people constitute American war crimes combined with the indiscriminate violence against Iraqi and Syrian civilians by the US military that caused the death of millions.*[336] Examples from some reported incidents: US forces massacred at least 25 unarmed Iraqi elderly, women, and children in the Haditha killings, raped a fourteen-year-old Iraqi girl then burned her alive before they killed her

---

[334] *Memorandum from Bracken and Davies to Talbot, June 20, 1963, DEF 19, box 2, Records of the Country Director, RG 59, USNA; Bass, Support Any Friend, 111.*

[335] *75 U.N.T.S. 287 (1949).*

[336] *Paragraph 358 of U.S. Army Field Manual 27-10 (1956)*

family in Mahmudiyah with the mercenaries and soldiers of this crime pardoned by Donald Trump. U.S. forces committed deplorable acts across Iraq such as the mass murder 42 unarmed Iraqi people at a wedding on the Iraqi Syrian border in the Mukaradeeb Wedding Massacre,[337] killed over 400 women and children sheltered in a school by American airstrike in the unlawful destruction of Raqqa that remains full of unreported war crimes along with Fallujah and the rest of Iraq and Syria, bombed over 278 unarmed civilians in Mosul by an American air raid that illegally employed white phosphorus, and all the violent raids of civilian homes.[338] The "war on terror" against a sectarian movement funded, trained, and armed by the U.S. remains within the framework of imperialist expansion as it aims to spread and benefit the military industrial complex.[339] Most recently in Iraq fifteen-year-old Zainab Essam Majed al-Khazali was murdered by the

---

[337] *Clark, Ramsey. War Crimes: A Report on United States War Crimes Against Iraq. United States, Maisonneuve Press, 1992.*

[338] *Human Rights Watch.Iraq/Syria: Danger from US White Phosphorus. © 2017 by Human Rights Watch.*

[339] *Proven US Is Protecting Al Qaeda In Syria – OpEd, 2018 WLNR 28478289*

U.S. military to the complete silence of the same media outlets that sensationalize the twenty-two-year-old Mahsa Amini[340]. Both of which took place around the same time to the condemnation by the supreme leader of Iran whom the U.S. has targeted with economic siege which violates the civil rights of Shi'ite Muslims in America.

II. The purposeful and indiscriminate fatalities, injuries, and destruction brought on by the invasion of Iraq constitute a breach to international humanitarian law:

As well as the illegality, the U.S. invasion committed a variety of **violations of** *international humanitarian law* (*IHL*), commonly referred to as the rules of armed conflict. IHL derives itself from several sources, including the four *1949 Geneva Conventions[341], the First Additional*

---

[340] *Killing of teenage Iraqi girl eposes western double standards, AL MAYADEEN ENGLISH, (Sept. 21, 2022) https://english.almayadeen.net/news/politics/us-occupation-forces-cold-bloodedly-kill-teenage-iraqi-girl.*

[341] *75 U.N.T.S. 135; 75 U.N.T.S. 287.*

Protocol to the 1949 Geneva Conventions[342], and the 1907 Hague Regulations (Protocol I).[343]

International Humanitarian Law ("IHL") lays forth the requirements for the behavior of occupation forces, limits the tools or methods permitted amid battle, and obliges parties to a violent conflict to protect civilians. IHL violations amount to war crimes. With the establishment of the Geneva Conventions[344] and the ratification of the War Crimes Act of 1996 for Protecting Civilians[345], the U.S. Congress explicitly added the 1949 Geneva Conventions into American law. Thus, it developed as the supreme law of the land. Even prior to the Geneva Conventions this standard was first established as "an act of Congress ought never to be construed to violate the law of nations, if any other possible construction remains". Quoted in: **Lauritzen v. Larsen 345 U.S. 571, 578, 73 S.Ct. 921,**

---

[342] *1125 U.N.T.S. 3..*

[343] *Convention (No. IV) Respecting the Laws and Customs of War on Land 1907, 2 AJIL Supp. (1908).*

[344] *75 U.N.T.S. 135; 75 U.N.T.S. 287.*

[345] *H.R. 3680, 104th Cong. (1996).*

926, 97 L.Ed. 1245 (1953)[346]. *The Charming Betsy,* 6 U.S. (2 Cranch), 34, 67, 2L.Ed. 208 (1904)[347]. The Supreme Court held that:

> "International law is part of our law and must be ascertained and administered by the Courts of justice of appropriate jurisdiction, as often as questions of right depending upon it are duly presented for their determination." *The Paquette Habana,* 175 U.S. 677, 700 (1900).[348]

Yet, the U.S. soldiers caused the deaths of over a million innocent civilians in Iraq alone, which directly breaches the IHL. The numerous military strategies and weapons account for the high civilian death toll. Unpredictable rocket attacks generated civilian casualties throughout Iraq and Syria and failed militarily according

---

[346] *Lauritzen v. Larsen, 345 U.S. 571, 73 S. Ct. 921, 97 L. Ed. 1254 (1953)*

[347] *Murray v. Schooner Charming Betsy, 6 U.S. 64 (1804)*

[348] *The Paquete Habana, 175 U.S. 677, 20 S. Ct. 290, 44 L. Ed. 320 (1900).*

to experts with the expenditure of trillions of US dollars and emboldened Iraqi Resistance movement. **Human Rights Watch reported in 2003 that the mass use of cluster bombs during the invasion along with many attempts to "decapitate" key Iraqi officials caused the deaths of many Iraqi civilians.**[349] An analogous conclusion was reached by the World Tribunal on Iraq. The use of napalm, firebombs, and indiscriminate use of depleted uranium, which emit hazardous waste and created long-term environmental concerns, also exposed Iraqi people to considerable damage.[350] The Proportion of children under 5 with leukemia saw an over 400% increase from 1990 to 2000, the incidence rate of malignant diseases witnessed a 300% increase from 1990 to 1999.[351] Cancer rates skyrocketed across Iraq so much so that the rate exceeds that of Hiroshima. The results in Syria will appear in the years to come but for now amid

---

[349] *Supra note 227, Off Target: The Conduct of the War and Civilian Casualties in Iraq.*

[350] *Ronald Kramer, Raymond Michalowski & Dawn Rothe, "The Supreme International Crime": How the U.S. War in Iraq Threatens the Rule of Law, 32 THE MANY FACES OF VIOLENCE 52 (2005).*

[351] *Cancer Reporting Center Maternity and Child Hospital, Basrah*

a global pandemic under the most coercive siege prevents importation of medicines and adequate irrigation and sanitation systems in addition to fertilizer for what was formerly an advanced system of agriculture to maintain what once was one of the best standards of livelihood in the world with free access to healthcare, education, and a reasonable cost of life.

Article 55: Protection of the Natural Environment[352]

Care shall be taken in warfare to protect the natural environment against widespread, long-term and severe damage. This protection includes a prohibition of the use of methods or means of warfare which are intended or may be expected to cause such damage to the natural environment and thereby to prejudice the health or survival of the population.

---

[352] *Protocol 1, Additional to the Geneva Convention*

Attacks against the natural environment by way of reprisals are prohibited.

The United Nations Security Council never approved the occupation of Iraq, a legal occupation cannot exist "the occupying power does not acquire any rights to sovereignty, land, or people."[353] The U.S. occupation had caused the deaths of roughly a million Iraqi and Syrian citizens, transformed the Syrian and Iraqi economy illegally, responded to the Iraqi resistance by genocidal tactics, torture, and abuse of Iraqi people. All of which failed to quell the national resistance movement that developed into the Popular Mobilization Forces that went on to swiftly defeat of the U.S. caliphate and place an end to the US combat mission in Iraq. These breaches of international humanitarian law raise the international responsibility of the U.S. officials behind the war Iraq. The arguments presented apply to US warfare against Syria. The United States conducted a missile attack on Shayrat

---

[353] *See Occupation and International Humanitarian Law: Questions and Answers, INTERNATIONAL COMMITTEE OF THE RED CROSS, (April 8, 2004) https://www.icrc.org/en/doc/resources/documents/misc/634kfc.htm.*

Airbase on April 7, 2017, then again in April of 2018[354], which belong to a string of direct military operations by American forces against the Syrian government and its allies. Trump declared the aim to keep a military presence in Syria to topple President Bashar al-Assad[355] and counter Iranian influence. Early in September 2018, the US launched a significant diplomatic effort to further its goals in Syria as part of a new strategy that attempted to indefinitely extend its military effort. Such use of force has no justification under international law, whether under Art. 51 of the UN Charter, humanitarian intervention, or chapter VII reply to the threat of international peace and security.

---

[354] *US, Britain, France launch air strikes in Syria (Updated), 2018 WLNR 11196077*

[355] *Report Claims Trump Wanted To Assassinate Syria's Assad. Eurasia Review February 16, 2021 Tuesday*

Figure 7: Syrian residence bombed by Israeli forces in Damascus near Sayyeda Zainab (AS) District

The United States violated Syrian sovereignty through several airstrikes before and after such as the 2018 attack that massacred over 100 Syrian soldiers in a single strike amid their fight against US militias in Deir al-Zor.[356] American approved Zionist aggression also continues regularly against Syria through assaults against civilian targets, the Syrian Arab Army, Hezbollah,

---

[356] *Ben Norton, **US escalates war in Syria, killing 100 government soldiers**, while Turkey ramps up assault - real news interview Ben Norton (2018), https://bennorton.com/us-escalates-war-syria-killing-100-government-soldiers-turkey/ (last visited Mar 20, 2019).*

IRGC, and Iraqi armed forces[357]. Israeli aggression against vital civilian infrastructure to the complete silence of the UN has emboldened the illegal occupation to continue to destroy sites that include civilian ports and airports more openly on a regular basis.[358] The Islamic Republic of Iran not only provided military support to defend the Syrian Arab Republic years after the violent intervention of the US alliance but also has remained committed to **UN Resolution 2642** through humanitarian assistance despite the severe international embargo against Iran.[359]

III. U.S. officials committed human rights breaches in Iraq and illegal US detention centers:

An Amnesty International report produced in 2004, stated that U.S. and British soldiers killed protestors and ordinary civilians, tortured them, bombarded residential neighborhoods, torched homes, and destroyed property

---

[357] *Fighting Between U.S. and "Iran-Backed Militias" Escalates in Syria. New York Times (August 26, 2022)*

[358] *Presstv, Iran to UN: US, Israel preventing Syria from returning to normal PressTV (2022), with-UN-envoy (last visited Nov 14, 2022).*

[359] *S.C. Res. 2642 (2002).*

in a failed attempt to subdue the resistance. In ordinary interactions with people, they also used excessive, deadly force despite the lack of any proof that these Iraqis committed any crimes. To eliminate revolutionary fighters, coalition forces employed chemical weapons, took hostages, made arbitrary arrests, and detained people for an extended period without charge or access to attorneys or a right to a fair trial. According to another report issued by the International Committee of the Red Cross (ICRC), about 99% of all prisoners held captive by American officials in the torture chambers at Abu Ghraib endured incarceration without any legal basis.[360]

A 53-page Pentagon study produced by American Major General Antonio Taguba in 2004 described "systematic and illegal" torture in the Abu Ghraib prison. Taguba discovered multiple examples of wanton crimes. Photos from CBS' "60 Minutes II" on April 28, 2004, showed physical and sexual assault of Iraqi prisoners at the facility by U.S. military personnel. As Marjorie Cohn – the executive vice president of the **U.S.**

---

[360] *Newsday 28, March Hamasaeed, S., & Nada, G. (2020). Iraq Timeline: Since the 2003 War. United States Institute of Peace, 29*

National Lawyers Guild – has pointed: "these actions are not merely repugnant to human dignity; they violate the **Convention Against Torture and Other Cruel, Inhuman or Degrading Treatment or Punishment.**[361] **The Convention against Torture and Other Cruel, Inhuman or Degrading Treatment or Punishment,** adopted by unanimous agreement of the United Nations General Assembly on December 10, 1984, and ratified by the United States on October 27th, 1990."[362]

Article 2 of the Convention Against Torture provides that: "Each State Party shall take effective legislative, administrative, judicial, or other measures to prevent acts of torture in any territory under its jurisdiction.[363] The second paragraph of the same Article adds that: "no exceptional circumstances whatsoever, whether a state of war or a threat of war, internal political instability, or any other public emergency, may be invoked as a justification of torture.[364] Finally, paragraph 3 of Art. 2. emphasizes

---

[361]   *1465 U.N.T.S. 85, 113.*

[362]   *Id.*

[363]   *Id.*

[364]   *Id.*

that "an order from a superior officer or a public authority may not be invoked as a justification of torture."[365] In fact soldiers possess a legal duty not to obey unlawful orders from their superiors.

Again, the **Convention Against Torture** not only internationally binds states, but also has the effect of federal law, thus established as the supreme law on the U.S. land.[366] As such, the U.S. directly breached the Convention Against Torture in Iraq, which raises the liability of U.S. soldiers involved alongside the vicarious liability of high-ranked U.S. officials in the Bush regime and other administrations who ordered such torture. The Taguba report and other governmental probes show the complicity of highly ranked state officials and private contractors recruited by the US.[367] "Personnel assigned to the 372nd MP Company, 800th MP Brigade were told to adjust facility procedures to prepare the environment for MI [military intelligence] interrogations", according to

---

[365] *Id.*

[366] *Id.*

[367] *Antonio Taguba, AR 15-6 Investigation of the 800th Military Police Brigade, DEPARTMENT OF DEFENSE, (Oct. 7, 2003) https://irp. fas.org/agency/dod/taguba.pdf.*

General Taguba.[368] The report proved that CIA agents, mercenaries, and Army intelligence requested MP guards to prepare the conditions for "favorable" interrogation of witnesses.[369]

The U.S. established a system of mass incarceration in Iraq to terrorize the population as part of a conspiracy to develop a world order directed against the poor and deprived with their human rights denied and placed in jail even if not tried.[370] The U.S. trial of former ally of Saddam Hussein was a direct breach to the right to fair trial pursuant to **Art. 14 of the International Covenant on Civil and Political Rights ("ICCPR")[371]. Article 14 (1) of the ICCPR provides that: "All persons shall be equal before the courts and tribunals. In the determination of any criminal charge against him, or of his rights and obligations in a suit at law, everyone shall be**

---

[368] *Id.*

[369] *Id.*

[370] *COUNTERINSURGENCY LESSONS FROM IRAQ, 2009 WLNR 30846254 "Iraq was essentially a police war"*

[371] *UN General Assembly, International Covenant on Civil and Political Rights, 16 December 1966, United Nations, Treaty Series, vol. 999, p. 171*

entitled to a fair and public hearing by a competent, independent, and impartial tribunal established by law." Article 14 of the ICCPR also provides for the presumption of innocence, the right to impartial and independent tribunal, and the proportionality of power between the litigants. The trial of Saddam Hussein never complied with **Art. 14 of the ICCPR**.[372] In fact, the trial practically breached every clause in Art. 14 of the ICCPR. The absence of power parity among the parties and lack of an impartial and independent tribunal constitutes two more blatant violations of the human right to a fair trial. The independence of the tribunal was compromised in all manifestations. Four of the five judges who presided over the cases faced removal that include two because of influence linked to the occupation authorities of the United States that was made public.[373] Four eminent world leaders warned the UN Secretary-General in a letter in September

---

[372] *Unpacking show trials: Situating the trial of Saddam Hussein. Harv. Int'l LJ, 48, 257.*

[373] *Tom Bowman, Saddam's Trial Halts; Judge May Be Removed, NORTH COUNTRY PUBLIC RADIO, (Sept. 14, 2006) https://www.northcountrypublicradio.org/news/npr/6076768/saddam-s-trial-halts-judge-may-be-removed.*

2005 about the danger posed to trial participants in Iraq such as torture. These cautions all met disregard despite proof of their occurrence. A few weeks later, two defense attorneys lost their lives to assassination in a way that raised questions about possible participation of the US coalition.[374] Afterwards, a potential defense witness was assassinated after US agents learned of his presence.[375] Even George Bush said the trial was proceeding as planned and that the Iraqi President will face execution. There was no presumption of innocence, no impartial judges, and no opportunity for an effective defense of an equal power. Simple money will highlight the power disparity. The prosecution of the Iraqi President has received hundreds of thousands of dollars in support from the United States, while the defense attorneys worked pro bono with just enough money to fly to Iraq.

Why should the President of Iraq face execution instead of architects of far greater violations of human rights and international law who face no trial whatsoever?

---

[374] *Becky Diamond, Two lawyers dead. Can Saddam trial take place?, NBC NEWS, (Nov. 8, 2005) https://www.nbcnews.com/id/wbna9968466.*

[375] *Saddam Lawyer Claims Witness Was Killed, FOX NEWS, (Na. 13, 2015) https://www.foxnews.com/story/saddam-lawyer- claims-witness-was-killed.*

The trial of Saddam Hussein on charges of Crimes Against Humanity necessitated transferal of the case over to Iraqi Resistance judicial processes free from US influence from start to finish. A comprehensive trial of the crimes owed to the people of Iraq will inevitably expose American engagement and complicity.[376] The U.S. relationship to the criminality of Saddam Hussein dates to early as 1959 when the CIA aided him in his failed assassination attempt of Abdel Karim Qassim,[377] followed by the 1963 coup when the CIA orchestrated mass executions of anyone even wrongly associated with communism.[378] Saddam was a major ally of the United States throughout 1980s[379] when some of the worst atrocities took place in Iraq in addition to the persecution and execution of the brilliant Shiite Muslim scholars of our era. The U.S. regime was

---

[376] *The Cost of War: Richard Falk*

[377] *Vincent Browne, Saddam may spill the beans, THE IRISH TIMES, (Dec. 17, 2003) https://www.irishtimes.com/opinion/saddam-may-spill-the-beans-1.400583.*

[378] *Richard Sanders, Regime Change: How the CIA put Saddam's Party in Power, (Oct. 24, 2002).*

[379] *Bruce Riedel, Lessons from America's First War with Iran, BROOKINGS, (May 22, 2013)*

integral to push Iraq to attack the Islamic Revolution in Iran. Afterwards in 1991, U.S. diplomats misled Saddam about their neutrality if he acted against Kuwaiti extraction of Iraqi oil after multiple attempts for peaceful negotiations.[380] The U.S. authorized his crackdown of the Kurdish people in the north whom Saddam Hussein granted autonomy. The U.S. furthermore oversaw the merciless suppression of the Arabs in the south of Iraq. Any wholistic trial of Saddam Hussein to settle grievances of the Iraqi people will expose the centrality of American imperialism in the condemned crimes.

Both the UN Special Rapporteur on the Independence of Judges and Lawyers in March 2006 and the UN Working Group on Arbitrary Detention on 30 November 2005 specifically stated that the United States and the imposed government shared responsibility for conducting the trial.[381] The trial has also

---

[380] *Elaine Sciolino & Michael R. Gordon, CONFRONTATION IN THE GULF; U.S. Gave Iraq Little Reason Not to Mount Kuwait Assault, N.Y. TIMES, (Sept. 23, 1990*

[381] *Jeremiah Lee, A Farce of Law: The Trial of Saddam Hussein, JURIST, (April 24, 2006) https://www.jurist.org/commentary/2006/04/farce-of-law-trial-of-saddam-hussein/.*

received criticism as an unjust process by human rights experts.[382] Leandro Despouy, the Special Rapporteur on the independence of judges and lawyers, wrote in his March 2006 report to the newly established Council on Human Rights that after his analysis and special concern since December 2003 at the time the Statute of the Iraqi Special Tribunal (IST) was recognized, and the Special Rapporteur spoke of his hesitation regarding the legality of the tribunal.[383]

IV. How to hold the US Officials Accountable for illegal warfare against Iraq and Syria?

International law faces challenges to hold the US and high-ranked government officials accountable before international law. **First, American officials refused to permanently sign on to the ICC Rome statute.**[384] Second, the US stands as a permanent member of the UN Security Council. As such, it possesses a veto power

---

[382] *Dougherty, B. (2004). Victims' justice, victors' justice: Iraq's flawed tribunal. Middle East Policy, 11(2).*

[383] *Supra note 293, Lee.*

[384] *2187 U.N.T.S. 90.*

to evade the ratification of any draft resolution to hold it accountable for its international supreme crimes in Iraq and Syria. **Article 36 (2) of the ICJ provides that: "the states parties to the present Statute may at any time declare that they recognize as compulsory ipso facto and without special agreement, in relation to any other state accepting the same obligation, <u>the jurisdiction of the Court in all legal disputes concerning the nature or extent of the reparation to </u> be made for the breach of an international obligation."**[385] Accordingly, Iraq can bring a dispute before the ICJ if the current US administration agrees to the ICJ jurisdiction with the support of a substantial mass struggle from civil society.[386] In 2003, the ICJ condemned the illegal invasion of Iraq for the lack of basis on any Security Council authorization,[387] yet it has yet to hold the U.S. officials accountable for the war in Iraq or Syria until we organize with tenacity

---

[385] *Statute of the International Court of Justice (1945), https://www. icj-cij.org/en/statute.*

[386] *Id.*

[387] *Arwa Mahdawi, Iraq war was illegal and breached UN charter, says Annan, THE GUARDIAN, (Sept. 15, 2004) https://www. theguardian.com/world/2004/sep/16/iraq.iraq.*

for the conditions that will allow this to take place. Legal resistance to subvert the US legal system against US officials suggests another defense strategy with the case law and statutes cited hereinto. **Nonetheless, we call for a viable solution to hold the US accountable for illegal war against the Republic of Iraq and Syrian Arab Republic.**

Establish an international specialized Court such as the Nuremberg Trials:

In the aftermath of World War II, An International Military Tribunal (IMT) in Nuremberg, Germany, was established by the allied forces who also formed the UN.[388] The Nuremberg tried top German officials faced trial for Nazi German war crimes, notably the Holocaust, after the World War II.[389] Twenty- two major Nazi officials appeared

---

[388] *The Nuremberg Trials, THE NATIONAL WWII MUSEUM, (last visited Jan. 12, 2023) https://www.nationalww2museum.org/war/topics/nuremberg-trials.*

[389] *The Nuremberg Trials, THE NATIONAL WWII MUSEUM, (last visited Jan. 12, 2023) https://www.nationalww2museum.org/war/topics/nuremberg-trials.*

before judges from the Allied powers.[390] After that, the US held 12 more trials in Nuremberg against highly-ranked members of the Nazi military, government, and SS as well as distinguished doctors and businessmen.[391] Crimes against peace, war crimes, crimes against humanity, and conspiracy to commit any of the crimes all faced trial before the Nuremberg courts.[392] A total of 199 defendants underwent prosecution at Nuremberg; 12 of them IMT defendants.[393] 161 faced charges as guilty.[394] If history still exists with the collapse of American imperialism which has global implications then humanity will likely view the American settler state in retrospect as the fascist global police state that it represented which will provide the opportunity to put U.S. state officials and military generals on trial.

---

[390] *Id.*

[391] *Id.*

[392] *61-74. Wright, Q. (1947). The law of the Nuremberg trial. American Journal of International Law, 41(1).*

[393] *Supra note 300, The Nurembereg Trials.*

[394] *61-74. Wright, Q. (1947). The law of the Nuremberg trial. American Journal of International Law, 41(1).*

Multiple specialized Tribunals to try war criminals developed throughout history. In addition to the **Tokyo War Crimes Trial (Resolution 1503 (XLVIII)),**[395] the UN established **the International Criminal Tribunal for Rwanda (ICTR) which suggested the complicity of media campaigns that aid in war crimes.** Such Tribunals report directly to the United Nations Security Council, rather than the various political movements involved, which means the criteria for these causes remain determined by the UN which failed to end U.S. war crimes. Specialized International Tribunals with the intention of trials for war criminals such as the **International Human Rights Tribunal Barcelona, International Tribunal of Indigenous Peoples and Oppressed Nations in the United States of America**, and the **Bertrand Russel Tribunals on US war against the Vietnamese people** broke the criminal silence in attempt to apply standards of international law for indictment of American federal and state officials. **Alien Tort Claim Act (ATCA) §1331**

---

[395] *38-72. Totani, Y. (2008). The Tokyo war crimes trial: The pursuit of justice in the wake of World War II (Vol. 299). Cambridge: Harvard University Asia Center.*

(Treaties and Laws of the U. S.)[396] grants nationals from any country the right to file claims and sue for international human rights violations in U.S. courts.[397] CACI International currently faces trial for complicity in the atrocities of Abu Ghraib.[398] The struggle to enact ATCA against the crimes of Western imperialism remains unaccomplished as the statute acts as a means for the US federal government to exercise jurisdiction across the entire planet. Universal jurisdiction provides another method for nations and peoples to prosecute and indict war criminals for international crimes if they travel within their jurisdiction. If revolutionary movements seize state power, or if civil society applies enough pressure for states to prosecute U.S. officials responsible for war crimes against Syria and Iraq, then this will aid the formation of an effective enforcement mechanism. In conjunction with all other strategies to investigate and imprison the greatest war criminals in human history. Universal jurisdiction suggests an alternative route from international tribunals or the ICC and

---

[396] *Blum, J. M., & Steinhardt, R. G. (1981). Federal Jurisdiction over International Human Rights Claims: The Alien Tort Claims Act after Filartiga v. Pena-Irala. Harv. Int'l. LJ, 22, 53.*

[397] *28 U.S.C. § 1350.*

[398] *Lawrence Hurley; U.S. Supreme Court rejects defense contractor's Abu Ghraib torture appeal, REUTERS, (June 28, 2021)*

their limitations. The Islamic Republic of Iran has issued an arrest warrant for Donald Trump which provides an example of what options exist for independent states committed to internationally agreed upon norms to check the lawlessness of American imperialism.[399]

---

[399] *Nada Al-Taher, Sam Kiley and Tara John, CNN Iran issues arrest warrant for Trump over drone strike that killed Qasem Soleimani*

Role Of The Media

The International Criminal Tribunal of Rwanda (ICTR) ruled on the "Rwanda Media Case" for the indictment of media executives that facilitate war efforts and promote genocide through sources of media *The Prosecutor v. Ferdinand Nahimana, Jean-Bosco Barayagwiza* and *Hassan Ngeze*, **Case No. ICTR-99-52**.[400] Media directors faced prosecution for genocide, complicity in genocide, direct and public incitement of genocide, conspiracy, crimes against humanity (extermination, persecution, murder), and cumulative charges and convictions. The ICTR asserted that the media administrators fully knew about the power of the media to inflame hatred and violence that causes mass murder of innocent civilians. The Judges of the ICTR

---

[400] *Article 38(1)(b) of the ICJ*

superficially ruled for limitations of free speech that induces crimes of genocide through various media outlets; broadcasts, television, publications, radio, and print.[401] If applied to serve oppressed nations rather than oppressor nations, the judgment to prevent the production of media that generates support for genocide marks an achievement of a standard that meets the time of mass communication despite the questionable basis and political nature of the case.

The tribunal warrants critical skepticism, but the judgment to prevent the production and exploitation of propaganda that fuels genocide through all platforms of media marks the achievement of an up-to-date standard in this technological age to protect the rights of nations and their human dignity. The politics of the court, however, suggests the interpretation of this principle will serve the interests of imperialism if we fail to act. Media dissemination remains monopolized by an elite board of directors in large financial institutions that distort news

---

[401] *International Criminal Tribunal for Rwanda, The Prosecutor v. Jean-Paul Akayesu (ICTR-96-4-T), Judgement of the Trial Chamber of 2 September 1998.*

to advance their interests and maintain the social order under colonial imperialism.[402] It was Western colonial rule over Rwanda that developed propaganda that obscures any class analysis to create the conditions of genocidal sectarian conflict just as it has in Iraq and Syria.

The United States has a history in the cover-up techniques in wars where imperialism spreads disinformation about other nations and looks for scapegoats to evade the blame. The US spread disinformation about the genocide in Rwanda to later provide cover for its military interventions in numerous countries that include Syria and Iraq. The Rwandan genocide traces itself to the manipulation of information by those in positions of government and non-government influence.[403] This means that the United States references the Rwandan Genocide to rationalize intervention under the guise of human rights it was complicit in the violation of in

---

[402] *McChesney; Robert Waterman. Rich Media, Poor Democracy: Communication Politics in Dubious Times. New Press, 2015.*

[403] *Garrison, Ann. "Et Tu, RT? Amplifying Western Disinformation on Rwanda." Black Agenda Report. Last modified November 7, 2018. https://blackagendareport.com/ et-tu-rt-amplifying-western-disinformation-rwanda.*

the first place. The idea that the United States failed to intervene and take action to prevent the genocide and therefore allowed for this crime to take place resembles the narrative on Syria and laid the groundwork for interventionist rationale. The mass violence was caused by covert American intervention, precisely because of American actions, not due to any lack of action. The propaganda that surrounds the events in Rwanda that has not faced prosecution or restrictions serves as the basis for the narrative that the US federal government needs to increase the mass production of missiles to attack nations like Syria or Iraq in the name of genocide prevention that it perpetrated in the first place.

States at war long understood the power of media to shape public perception and manipulate the narrative. They employ various tactics, through intelligence agencies like the FBI and CIA to control disinformation campaigns, such to control independent news sources or establish media relations units, to use journalism for their own purposes. Propaganda, mechanisms to brainwash, and other forms of persuasion commonly used in armed conflicts, and the media functions at every stage to serve imperialism.[404] Before hostilities begin, the media mobilizes and persuades public opinion. During the conflict, it conceals and galvanizes, and after the conflict it legitimizes state actions and shapes public perception of the victory while censorship of any criticism.

A leaked document from the International Criminal Tribunal for Rwanda (ICTR) shows that the US supported the Rwandan Patriotic Front (RPF), an armed faction that entered Rwanda from Uganda that initiated acts of violence against the Rwandan people and government for four years. Yet the ICTR defined the imposed conflict in Rwanda as a civil war even though the US intervened and backed an invasion into the country that committed human rights abuses with impunity in violation of the Leahy laws yet again. So why was the decision of Saddam to invade Kuwait not considered a civil war?[405] In both cases the indigenous elements, whether Saddam or

---

[404] *Southwell, Brian G., Emily A. Thorson, and Laura Sheble, eds. Misinformation and mass audiences. University of Texas Press, 2018.*

[405] *Herman, E. S., Peterson, D. (2014). Enduring Lies: The Rwandan Genocide in the Propaganda System, 20 Years Later. Indonesia: Real News Books.*

Nahimana, faced prosecution without any presumption of innocence for war crimes instead of the administrators and enforcers of the imperialist alliance that engineered those violations. Despite the fact of an asymmetry in power relations between imperialism and the proxy elements it empowers and enables. By 1994, they launched a final attack and violently seized power by massacres of innocent lives. This report used as evidence at the ICTR revealed that the Tutsi RPF committed countless murders in different parts of Rwanda with the help of the CIA.[406] Evidence from the report shows that Paul Kagame, the then leader of the Front and current Rwandese president, was involved in the destruction of a plane that carried the former Rwandese and Burundian presidents with other military officials and the subsequent genocide.[407] Yet the

---

[406] *Reyntjens, Filip. "The RPF did it: a fresh look at the 1994 plane attack that ignited genocide in Rwanda." Working papers/ University of Antwerp. Institute of Development Policy and Management; Université d'Anvers. Institut de politique et de gestion du développement.-Antwerp (2020).*

[407] *AU, RASSEMBLEMENT REPUBLICAIN POUR LA DEMOCRATIE. "Press release No. 4/2003: War crimes committed by the RPF should be investigated and prosecuted by the ICTR in Rwanda." (2003).*

eventual rule of Kagame never faced any sanctions unlike the genocidal siege Iraq suffered with the complicity of the UN and international courts. Several officials, such as the Kagame Chief of Staff, testified that Kagame ordered the RPF military to shoot down the plane with authorization from the US federal government that wanted to control Centrak African resources through support for the Tutsi RPF by proxy. [408] A former RPF intelligence officer outlined that Bill Clinton was personally responsible for the attack which makes him subject to criminal indictment just as every other American president. The US federal government assassinated Habyarimana to enable the transformation of Rwanda into an American client state under the rule of Kagame.[409] Clinton conspired with Paul Kagame and Yoweri Museveni to push Mobutu for secession out of the Democratic Republic of Congo to facilitate American control of Congolese minerals

---

[408] *Black, "Top Secret: Rwanda War Crimes Cover-Up."*

[409] *Madsen, Wayne. Genocide and covert operations in Africa, 1993-1999. Vol. 50. Lewiston, NY: Edwin Mellen Press, 1999.*

and to reverse the drive towards national independence spearheaded by Patrice Lumumba[410].

The political nature of the Court that ruled the Rwandan Media Case especially raises questions given the silence on the genocide that unfolded in the Democratic Republic of Congo. The missiles used to attack the aircraft of President Habyarimana which the ICRT never prosecuted belonged to weapons that the United States seized from the mass murder it committed in the first Iraq gulf war. The CIA smuggled the armaments through Uganda into a weapons manufacturing warehouse in Kigali, controlled by a Western intelligence front company.[411] A legal investigation informed Boutros-Boutros Ghali, the Secretary-General of the UN in 1994, of CIA complicity in the crime.[412] This evidence further

---

[410] *Id.*

[411] *Kuzmarov, Jerem. "Still Unsolved: the Great Crime That Triggered the 1994 Rwandan Genocide." Black Agenda Report. Last modified April 7, 2021. https://www.blackagendareport.com/ still-unsolved-great-crime-triggered-1994-rwandan- genocide*

[412] *Garrison, Ann. "Et Tu, RT? Amplifying Western Disinformation on Rwanda." Black Agenda Report. Last modified November 7, 2018. https://blackagendareport.com/ et-tu-rt-amplifying-western-disinformation-rwanda.*

supported the claim American intervention, not the lack of intervention, was central for what transpired in Rwanda. Yet the Rwanda Media Case ruled in favor of the victor against members of the historically marginalized class. America was involved in the genocide by additional assistance to train RPF members in missile attacks in Arizona.[413] In a document titled **"General Report on the Special Investigations concerning the crimes committed by the Rwanda Patriotic Army (RPA) during 1994,"** presented by the prosecution during the ICTR genocide trial, detailed accounts of horrific crimes against Hutu refugees by the RPF. The document contains information about the group that hunted down Hutus in the Democratic Republic of Congo through spotter planes with US identification as part of an unspoken genocide immune from prosecution.[414]

The production of propaganda to facilitate selective war crimes led to the indictment of three media executives

---

413 *Kuzmarov, "Still Unsolved: the Great Crime That Triggered the 1994 Rwandan Genocide."*

414 *Rever, Judi. In praise of blood: The crimes of the Rwandan Patriotic Front. Vintage Canada, 2020.*

in the case of ***Prosecutor v. Ferdinand Nahimana, Jean-Bosco Barayagwiza, and Hassan Ngeze***. This case involved the conviction of the three defendants for (1) genocide; (2) direct and public incitement to commit genocide; and (3) persecution as a crime against humanity based upon the responsibility for incendiary radio broadcasts and newspaper articles.[415] The trial chamber of the International Criminal Tribunal for Rwanda (ICTR) convicted Ferdinand Nahimana and Jean-Bosco Barayagwiza for their involvement in the infamous *Radio Télévision Libre des Mille Collines* (RTLM), which allegedly incited and directed the 1994 genocide in Rwanda. The third defendant, Hassan Ngeze, was convicted for his position as the editor-in-chief of the newspaper *Kangura*.

The trial chamber in this case established three crucial tests that apply to determine whether media executives had facilitated genocide or war. These tests, a) the intent test b) content test (c) consequence test established themselves to determine the accountability of media in the inducement

---

[415] *Orentlicher, Diane F. "Criminalizing hate speech in the crucible of trial: Prosecutor v. Nahimana." Am. U. Int'l L. Rev. 21 (2005): 557.*

of genocidal war crimes.[416] Upon analysis of these tests, it remains clear that they require urgent application to imperial powers that produce complicated and sophisticated propaganda as accomplices to human rights violations. The United States, in continued invasions, capitalizes off the press through the media houses that contribute to the national economy.[417] Therefore, US media coverage of American invasions has a component of mass deceit, manipulation, control, and propaganda to demonize the oppressed and humanize the oppressor. As Javed Huma and Arshi Hashmi outlined, the mainstream media in the United States conforms to the government philosophy in terms of formulation and distribution of

---

[416] *Davidson, H. Ron. "The International Criminal Tribunal for Rwanda's Decision in The Prosecutor v. Ferdinand Nahimana et al.: The Past, Present, and Future of International Incitement Law." Leiden Journal of International Law 17, no. 3 (2004): 505-519.*

[417] *Kellner, Douglas. "Spectacle and media propaganda in the war on Iraq: A critique of US broadcasting networks." Yahya Kamalipour et al.(Hg.): War, Media, and Propaganda. A Global Perspective, Lanham: Rowman & Littlefield (2004): 69*

news to fabricate and win the hearts and minds of local and international audiences[418].

Evidence has emerged to prove that the American federal government was instrumental to the genocide that took place in Rwanda but deliberately kept this information hidden conceal their complicity.[419] Just as it has in both and covert operations against Iraq and Syria. The Clinton administration that bombed Iraq on a regular basis possessed the information from the different government and military institutions to oversee the genocide in Rwanda.[420] Moreover, after immediately after the premeditated murder of President Habyarimana orchestrated by the US military, the United States closed all embassies and evacuated all American citizens from

---

[418] *Javed, Huma, and Arshi Saleem Hashmi. "Corporate Media Manipulation in the U.S. Wars: A Case Study of Iraq War." Margalla Papers 25, no. 1 (2021): 147.*

[419] *Epstein, Helen C. "America's Secret Role in the Rwandan Genocide." The Guardian. Last modified September 12, 2017. https://www.theguardian.com/news/2017/sep/12/americas-secret-role-in-the-rwandan-genocide.*

[420] *The US and the genocide in Rwanda 1994: Information, intelligence and the US response. National Security Archive, 2001.*

Rwanda[421]. Therefore, we conclude that the failure to intervene was a disguised narrative to hide their illegal decision to intervene as an accomplice to genocide. The supposed remorse expressed by Bill Clinton and the subsequent vow to prevent future genocides by the invasion of Iraq and Syria was a facade to conceal the American association in the genocide in Rwanda and provide a cover for future interventions. The US government intended to absolve itself from involvement and instead shift the focus to their efforts towards imperialist action in the name of humanitarianism with public support manipulated by the mass media. The response of the US federal government to the Rwanda genocide was nothing but deceit with the assistance of the media that helped build the narrative for subsequent military interventions in Iraq and Syria.[422]

Despite the evidence available - the Western alliance never faced accountability for their involvement in Rwanda by any international court which undermines the

---

[421] *Braeckman, Collette. "New York and Kigali." New Left Review (2001): 141.*

[422] *Language, media manipulation, and the "war on terror", by Normon Solomon*

legitimacy of the Rwanda Media Case despite the valid need to restrict mass deceit through media conglomerates.[423] Instead, Hutu community members, such as the three African journalists in the case of *Prosecutor v. Ferdinand Nahimana, Jean-Bosco Barayagwiza, and Hassan Ngeze*, faced prosecution[424]. The thousands of innocent men, women, and children killed by the Western backed RPF never attained justice through any court that serves the rich and powerful. The U.S. media has turned international justice into a facade and given perpetrators of genocide against Africa to West Asia immunity from accountability.

The ICTR will argue in defense of the decision that the court clarified that it seeks to apply more restrictive enforcement of speech that reinforces the power of the state rather than that which challenges it has less legal protection. However, this sidesteps the nature of the state and whether it serves the interests of imperialism and exploitation or asserts the right to self-determination.

---

[423] *Politics of the media Giants (McChesney's Rich Media, Poor Democracy)*

[424] *Prosecutor v. Nahimana,* **2003 I.C.T.R. 99 (2003).**

The establishment media historically understates or ignores certain facts such as the number of casualties caused by the US federal government and instead focuses on issues and fabrications that win popular support.[425] Government officials apply pressure on journalists to self-censor legally significant facts that incriminate the US government officials for major war crimes especially since the exposure of the My Lai massacre that provoked robust anti-imperialist organization and international tribunals that threatened the power structure. This makes the mainstream press an author or accomplice of these unaccounted crimes against the nations like Iraq and Syria pursuant to the standard that legal assistance to the oppressed will argue in favor from Rwanda Media Case.

In the Nahimana case, one of the arguments of the prosecutions was that the journalists spread hate speech and incited the Hutus against the Tutsis. If we apply this argument to the US media that propagated the wars on Iraq and Syria, media channels incited violence against the Iraqi and Syrian people for the US invasions. On

---

[425] *Global media, neoliberalism and imperialism, by Robert McChesney*

the 20th of March 2003, America militarily invaded Iraq after decades of exhaustion through wars, blockades, biological warfare, and massacres. Long before the 2003 ground invasion, the U.S. administration via the media publicly condemned Iraq, rejected any diplomatic efforts, and escalated U.S. aggression. The corporate media was concerned with the demonization of Iraq. The U.S. administration used the media to dehumanize the Iraqi people and not portray them as ordinary humans to reclaim American hegemony and kick the Vietnam Syndrome. In a Washington Post column decades ago, Marjorie Williams published an article against the Iraqi Republic. Several other media outlets fabricated reports that the Iraqi military started to kill people at ten years old by shooting them at the back and burning their bodies in acid.[426] George Bush defended his escalation of aggression by false accusations that Saddam Hussein was involved in the attacks of September 11th, and that Iraq failed to comply with the UN requirements

---

[426] *"The Iraq Syndrome: Demonic Victims and Angelic Demons." Welcome to Third World Network (TWN). Accessed January 20, 2023. https://twn.my/title/twr147b.htm.*

for inspections of weapons of mass destruction. Bush baselessly claimed Iraq still possessed weapons of mass destruction that he intended to use against the United States and transfer to so called terrorist organizations to incite fear and hate amongst the American population. Many believed these allegations against Iraq due to the influence of well-funded media. However, subsequent research shows that these claims amounted to lies yet no one has faced consequences unlike the Rwanda Media Case. Nothing was found with regards to weapons of mass destruction in Iraq nor association to terrorism.[427] Media publications, such as journalist articles by Judith Miller, which alleged inaccurate information about weapons of mass destruction, significantly impacted America to the extent that officials in the Bush administration used it as

---

[427] *Datta, Arko. "CIA's Final Report: No WMD Found in Iraq." NBC News. Last modified April 25, 2005. https://www.nbcnews.com/id/wbna7634313.*

a cover for the war on Iraq.[428] The New York Times, where Miller worked, was also criticized for the fabrication of Iraqi weapons of mass destruction as fact without enough evidence. This shows how the inclination of these news sources to manipulation and misinformation led to innumerable atrocities in Iraq. The US military employed chemical weapons in the guise of their removal.

Similarly, CNN used a fake activist of Syrian origin to justify the war in Syria.[429] CNN, like most mainstream media channels disseminates fictitious footages from Syria to lay the groundwork for military intervention. In a leaked online video, an individual named Danny fabricates a video broadcast for CNN. Before the video, he asks some of his colleagues to fire weapons for a dramatic effect in

---

[428] *See Miller, J. (2001), A nation challenged: Secret Sites; Iraqi Tells of Renovations at Sites for Chemical and Nuclear Arms, The New York Times. See also: Miller, J. (2003), After effects: Prohibited Weapons; Illicit Arms Kept Till Eve of War, An Iraqi Scientist Is Said to Assert, The New York Times. Accessed 20/01/23: http://www.nytimes.com/2003/04/21/world/aftereffects-prohibited-weapons-illicit-arms-kept-till-eve-war-iraqi-scientist.html*

[429] *"One Activist's Chronicle of Daily Hell in Syria." This Just In - CNN.com Blogs. Last modified February 13, 2012. https://news.blogs.cnn.com/2012/02/13/one-activists-chronicle-of-daily-hell-in-syria/comment-page-2/.*

his live coverage with Anderson Cooper. A multitude of videos online show supposed casualties killed by a "chemical attack" who walked away once they thought that the videos ended. Western media designed these fabrications so that the US alliance build a pretext for a legitimate reason to wage war on Syria. In April 2018, the British Broadcasting Company aired a documentary video that was widely distributed across the globe. The footage depicted children and civilians in a state of distress, hosed down and gasped for air, as an announcer breathlessly narrated that these accounted for the atrocities committed by Syrian forces loyal to President Bashar al-Assad. The documentary also featured testimony from opposition witnesses who claimed that chemical weapons dropped from the sky, which caused many deaths and left countless more injured[430]. In application of the content test applied in the *Nahimana* case, the content of Western media footage fails the test; thus, this corporation needs to face accountability. The content test checks the language

---

[430] *New Worlds. "BBC Admits Fake News, Syria Did Not Gas Its People." The Manila Times. Last modified September 22, 2021. https://www.manilatimes.net/2021/09/19/opinion/columns/bbc-admits-fake-news-syria-did-not-gas-its-people/1815246.*

and words used by the media and whether they link to violence. One week after the video broadcasted by the Western press, the US adhered to the portrayed narrative and launched more than one hundred missiles on Syria without sufficient and credible evidence, which killed innocent civilians. These attacks continue. After three years, the British news company was compelled to admit that the information presented in the video was false and retracted their statements. If the standard in *Nahimana* and *Sürek v. Turkey (No. 1)* was applied, Western media channels that went with such narratives cannot escape prosecution for content that led to the death of innocent Syrians. In an interview with Anhar Kochneva, director of a Moscow-based tourist firm specialized in West Asia, it was revealed that contrary to what the Western media portrayed, most Syrians support of President Assad. RT journalist, Kochneva highlighted, "*There are many vehicles with the president's portraits driving the streets throughout the country – ranging from old, barely moving crankers to brand new Porsches and Hummers. You can't force people into hanging up portraits. It means that people support the president rather than the rebellion.*"[431] The media often posted videos and photos of Syrians protests loyal to the president and presented them as opposition protests. Reports also show that after the United States invaded Iraq, they tried to incite sectarian violence between Sunni and Shi'i Muslims to divide the country in attempt to prevent the unified struggle that effectively combatted the invasion.

The case of *Holder v. the Humanitarian Law Project* demonstrates the vilification of Muslims under the guise of the war against terrorism. While the media has the free speech protection under the First Amendment, organizations that supported the PKK faced accusations as foreign terrorist organizations. *Holder v. The Humanitarian Law Project* was a Supreme Court case that dealt with the scope of the material support provision of the Patriot Act. The Humanitarian Law Project, a non-profit organization, tried to provide support to the Kurdistan Workers' Party (PKK) and the Liberation Tigers of Tamil Eelam (LTTE),

---

[431] *Kevorkova, Nadezhda. "Western Media Lie About Syria – Eyewitness Reports." RT International. Last modified April 29, 2011. https://www.rt.com/news/syria-lies-interview/.*

in the form of peaceful resolution of disputes and human rights advocacy. The government argued that this support provided material assistance to a terrorist organization, which the despotic Patriot Act outlawed. The Supreme Court ultimately ruled in favor of the government and held that the material support provision of the Patriot Act was constitutional because the type of support that the Humanitarian Law Project attempted to provide was material assistance to a designated terrorist organization. The Court noted that even if the support was intended for peaceful, lawful activities, it still might free up other resources of the organization to engage in so called terrorist activities. The Patriot Act, of which the material support provision belongs to, clearly targets Muslim individuals and organizations discriminatorily.

It remains difficult to understate the misguidance of the U.S. media in the wars in Iraq and Syria. The presentation of false statements and events displayed as true amounts to a criminal offense. In the case of *New York Times v. Sullivan*, an advertisement in The New York Times that criticized the treatment of civil rights activists in Alabama - L. B. Sullivan, a commissioner of

Montgomery, Alabama, claimed that the advertisement defamed him[432]. The New York times confirmed that they published information without the guarantee of accuracy. Although the media channel admitted to these facts, the U.S. Supreme Court, contrary to the decision made in the Nahimana case, refused to hold New York Times accountable. In a commentary on the domestic legal system of Cameroon, the United Nations Human Rights Committee (UNHRC) highlighted that, *"the prosecution and punishment of journalists for the crime of publication of false news merely on the grounds, without more, that the news was false, (is a) clear violation of Article 19 of the Covenant (ICCPR)."*[433] In support of this provision, Article 4 of the International Convention on the Elimination of All Forms of Racial Discrimination (CERD) demands that states take steps to prohibit any form of propaganda that promotes racial superiority. Any idea that says some

---

[432] *See New York Times Co. v. Sullivan, 376 U.S. 254, 84 S. Ct. 710, 11 L. Ed. 2d 686 (1964).*

[433] *Consideration of reports submitted by States Parties under Article 40 of the Covenant: Concluding observations of the Human Rights Committee. CCPR/C/79/Add.116. November 1999. Para 24. http://www.refworld.org/pdfid/3ae6b01014.pdf*

people of white European descent hold superiority over others because of their nationality amounts to racism. It amounts to racism whether Nazis, the KKK, or Zionism proclaim it. The convention also requires states to take measures to eliminate any incitement to racial discrimination and violence, and to prohibit any support for racist activities, that extends financial assistance. The US media undoubtedly spread propaganda to incite the public to wage war on Iraq and Syria. The US media demonized the Iraqi and Syrian people as inhuman terrorists to desensitize the world to their mass murder yet none of the American news source ever faced any trials for the devastation in direct contrast with the RTLM and Kagura who allegedly attacked the Tutsi ethnic minority with consequences. Therefore, the Nahimana case needs application universally as precedent to these imperialist forces that use their media as a tool to spread propaganda and misinformation to incite public support for genocide.

The US has waged psychological warfare to control ideas and thoughts [434] in the minds of the masses to

---

[434] *Franklin H. B. (2000). Vietnam and other American fantasies. University of Massachusetts Press.*

counteract revolutionary consciousness for centuries especially more recently in the wake of decolonial processes and technological advances in mass communication.[435] As early as the 1800s US representatives stated "We have, a far as possible, closed every avenue by which the light may enter the slave's mind. If we could extinguish the capacity to see the light, our work will be complete".[436] The US media inverts reality through the presentation of advances achieved by resistance movements as their losses and losses of the US military as victories.[437] Media dissemination remains monopolized by an elite board of directors in major financial institutions that distort news to advance their interests and maintain the status quo under colonial imperialism.[438] Colonial imperialism simply means the division of the international world stage

---

[435] *Seize the Time. Vol. 2, No. 1, May 1975*

[436] *Berry, Henry. "Fact Check: Quotes from Prominent American Statesmen on Race Are Accurate." Reuters, Thomson Reuters, 6 July 2020, https://www.reuters.com/article/uk-factcheck-quotes-statesmen-race/fact-check-quotes-from prominent- american-statesmen-on-race-are-accurate-idUSKBN2471YA.*

[437] *Seize the Time. Vol. 2, No. 1, May 1975.*

[438] *McChesney, Robert Waterman. Rich Media, Poor Democracy: Communication Politics in Dubious Times. New Press, 2015.*

into oppressive settler colonial nations whose elite classes of capitalists own monopoly corporations that oppress and super exploit the labor and natural resources of oppressed Third World nations. Morgan Finance Capital Group and Scripps Howard alone owns much of the mass media networks and thereby control the disinformation narrative that suppresses facts to deceive public opinion into support or apathy towards US and NATO violations of international law. It was European colonial rule over Rwanda that exasperated tensions between the ethnic groups of Hutus and Tutsis yet the court declared that this divide was intensified by Radio Television does Mille Coulines (RTLM) and the Kagura newspaper to the point of violent discord to disguise American complicity.

The US media has no right to take recourse to freedom of expression as a cover to manufacture support for mass slaughter across Iraq and Syria while it restricts the freedom of expression of Iraqi Resistance. The American government itself restricts the freedom of the press exercised by alternative sources of media that present facts about worldwide developments. The right to free speech requires contextual analysis but was not meant to protect violent threats and hateful incitement of mass murder. Many realize that neither the Syrian nor Iraqi people ever attacked the US or the West. So how can the media shamelessly justify the occupation of our lands with narratives that lack any factual basis? The invasion of Iraq was never motivated to protect the United States nor to protect the Iraqi people as the massacres perpetrated by the occupation exceed too many to count.[439] It was never intended protect the freedom of Americans who lost their civil liberties in the name of national security that deteriorated because of terrorism sponsored by foreign and domestic agendas in the expansion of this militarized police state.[440] It was never meant to aid the Iraqi people or show compassionate concern for their lives as the life of our nation was vastly favorable before the invasion with its criminal military machine that has no mercy on child,

---

[439] *See John Chapman, The real reasons Bush went to war, THE GUARDIAN, (July 27, 2004) https://www.theguardian.com/world/2004/jul/28/iraq.usa.*

[440] *Malang B.S. Bojang, The Hidden Agenda Behind the Invasion of Iraq: The Unjust War Over Iraq in 2003, 2 CENTRAL EUROPEAN JOURNAL OF POLITICS 1 (2016).*

woman, or senior[441] who previously lived in stability with free access to education and a modern universal healthcare system across Iraq and Syria. Journalists who covered atrocities committed by the US federal government risked assassination and dismissal from their positions for reports of the indiscriminate violence.[442]

After the experience of Iraq that lead to military losses and a domestic anti-war movement,[443] the techniques for the expansion of the war into Syria shifted into a covert nature that relies on soft media war to distort the public consciousness of targeted populations and proxy armies rather than boots on the ground. The financiers of corporate media exploited both the misery they inflict onto Syrians and the empathy of anyone effected to push for US regime change. Today social media has developed a new platform for mind control under the delusion of inverted realities

---

[441] *Iraq war veteran Jeff Engle Hart testifies that the US military ordered soldiers to "shoot anything that moves" in Fallujah*

[442] *Malang B.S. Bojang, The Hidden Agenda Behind the Invasion of Iraq: The Unjust War Over Iraq in 2003, 2 CENTRAL EUROPEAN JOURNAL OF POLITICS 1 (2016).*

[443] *Victoria Carty, The Anti-war Movement Versus the War Against Iraq, 14 INTERNATIONAL JOURNAL OF PEACE STUDIES 17 (2009).*

through analytic services such as Cambridge Analytica. The British firm collected personal data of Facebook users by the millions without their consent to advertise imperialist political agendas that involve Iraq and Syria. International criminal law first assessed the relationship between media and mass slaughter in 1946 when Julius Strecher, publisher of an anti-Semitic newspaper, was sentenced to death. Yet no such justice has emerged for the Third World. The portrayal of the Iraqi and Syrian people as terrorists despite the absence of ISIS prior to the invasion rationalized military orders to indiscriminately attack civilian populations with chemical weapons. All to the silence of the media which functions as a critical component of imperialism that incited these chemical attacks in the guise of chemical weapons removal.

The same media that misreported the events in Iraq has no credibility in the coverage of Syria.[444] The lack

---

[444] *See Michael E. O'Hanlon, Misplaced Blame: The Media's Performance in Iraq, BROOKINGS (April 11, 2006) https:// www.brookings.edu/opinions/misplaced-blame-the-medias-performance-in-iraq/; Jim Wolf, U.S. media curtail Iraq war coverage: study, REUTERS (Aug. 19, 2007) https://www.reuters. com/article/us-usa-iraq-media/u-s-media-curtail-iraq- war-coverage-study-idUSN1923063520070820.*

of coverage for massacres of Syrians when they fail to advance Western interests (i.e. Foua & Kafraya) proves that the moral outcry for Syrians allegedly killed by the government targeted by NATO reflects a cynical attempt to capitalize off Syrian suffering.[445] Especially given how Western media counts opposition fighters as civilian casualties.[446] Iraq & Syria therefore strikes the oppressive U.S. system the world remains subject to while the commercial media maintains a conspiracy of silence over these developments that encourage acts of defiance. The imperialist media tries to conceal the legal right to self-determination as terrorism and illegal imperialist actions as democratic law and order.[447] The corporate media censors the reality of anti- imperialist struggle and its advances in attempt to hide the voice of

---

[445] *Scott Lucas, The International Media is Failing to Report the Syrian War Properly, THE CONVERSATION, (Feb. 9, 2015) https://theconversation.com/the-international-media-is-failing-to-report-the-syrian-war-properly-37290.*

[446] *Syrian Observatory of Human Rights founded and lead by one British intelligence officer*

[447] *Eric C. Anderson, Confusing a "Revolution" with "Terrorism", SMALL WARS JOURNAL, (Jan. 19, 2015) https://smallwarsjournal. com/jrnl/art/confusing-a- "revolution"-with-"terrorism".*

the Iraqi Resistance not only in the mainland but also in the diaspora in America which violates civil and human rights.[448] US media attempts to hide their defeats through use of smoke screens and deception to distract the public from full awareness of US military and governmental vulnerabilities to save the morale and legitimacy of the American regime.[449] The US has spent billions on think tanks to develop methods for indoctrination to repress consciousness that unites oppressed people in the struggle against the US imperialism as witnessed in 1983 Beirut which shattered the illusion of American invincibility.[450]

Propaganda campaigns seek to blind us from political struggle that effectively challenge the power structure that profits off our suffering to instead brainwash and pollute

---

[448] *Al-Rashideen Army http://www.al-rashedeen.net/index.php/ articles/8-media-of-iraqi-resistance-is-the-second-pit.html*

[449] *Howard Kurtz, Media's failure on Iraq still stings, CNN (March 11, 2013) https://www.cnn.com/2013/03/11/opinion/kurtz-iraq-media-failure/index.html.*

[450] *PFLP Bulletin – Winter 1983. From Beirut to Grenada pg. 4*

our minds into passive defeatism and submission.[451] Propaganda platforms that serve as associates in the crimes of the Pentagon that introduced the war plan to cause a sense of "shock and awe" onto Iraq and the entire Arab region through lawless airstrikes against Baghdad. US media assisted the war crimes defined by article 6(b) of the 1945 Nuremberg Charter in the unjustified wanton destruction of the Iraqi capital. The establishment press served as an associate in major international crimes in a variety of ways like the incitement to illegal acts of violence in the public 48-hour ultimatum broadcasted to the world in violation of the customary international laws of war established in the 1907 Hague Convention on the Opening of Hostilities to which the United States was still a party in contract as proven through paragraphs 20, 21, 22, and 23 of the US Army Field Manual 27-10 (1956). In addition to all the crimes in decades prior, by the outset of the war of aggression against Iraq which possessed neither

---

[451] *Compare David Klepper, War via Tiktok: Russia's new tool for propaganda machine, AP NEWS, (Feb. 26, 2022) https:// apnews.com/article/russia-ukraine-technology-europe-media-nationalism-2186dbc533560cb666f59655ecf1e e8e.*

weapons of mass destruction nor any ties to the 9/11 attacks, the controlled press promoted crimes against peace as defined by the Nuremberg Charter (1945), Judgment (1946), Principles (1950) in addition to paragraph 498 of US Army Field Manual 27-10 (1956).[452] The media failed to honestly portray information and allow equal access to information necessary for full participation in any real democracy they proclaim.[453] Monopoly corporations and U.S. imperialism control the mass media even social media to bring the public mind under the ownership of the same U.S. elite that owns the rest of the economy.[454] They withhold "classified information" to benefit and protect corporate interests of powerful lobbies in Washington DC and push for laws that criminalize their publication and

---

[452] *Francis A. Boyle, Iraq and the Laws of War CounterPunch. org (2005), https://www.counterpunch.org/2005/12/22/ iraq- and-the-laws-of-war/.*

[453] *Steven Kull, Clay Ramsay & Evan Lewis, Misperceptions, the Media, and the Iraq War, 118 POLITICAL SCIENCE QUARTERLY 569 (2003).*

[454] *Ashley Lutz, These 6 Corporations Control 90% Of the Media in America, BUSINESS INSIDER, (June 14, 2012) https://www. businessinsider.com/these-6-corporations-control-90-of-the- media-in-america-2012-6.*

to monopolize media platforms i.e. Telecommunications Act of 1996.[455] We cannot change the character of the conglomerated media without fundamental change of the character of the whole system from which it emerges. The world must know and understand international events and the laws that govern them: what the US government tries to eradicate, why, and how to end this for the restoration of harmony and internationalist emancipation from worldwide imperialism.

Contrary to what American media displayed as an overthrow of the Iraqi Ba'athists with ease, the besieged Iraqi military displayed defiance across Iraq, although the imperialist media hid the reality of the conflict to demoralize resistance.[456] The Pentagon media machine covered the fact that dozens of US soldiers died in a single day when the Iraqi Republican Guard repelled them

---

[455] *United States v. Swartz, 945 F. Supp. 2d 216 (D. Mass. 2013)*

[456] *"Defeat Colonial Occupation of Iraq U.S. Imperialism Get the Hell out!". Wanton Imperialist Slaughter and Bitter Iraqi Resistance. The Internationalist. May-June 2003.*

in Nasriya.[457] A physician who travelled with a combat evacuation team later described the scene:

"U.S. led coalition tanks were burning alongside the road. On the north side of town we found the site of the ambush. It was hard to miss: three destroyed amphibious personnel carriers - also known as Amtracks - were burning."[458]

A corporal injured in Nasriya said U.S. command misled the army to expect mass desertions, however when they tried to reach the city, "it was a whole different ball game. They weren't rolling over like we thought they would."[459] A brigade commander in the Army's Third Division spoke of the ambushes, sniping, and suicide

---

[457] *See Calvin Woodward, U.S. soldiers captured, THE GADSDEN TIMES, (March 23, 2003), https://www.gadsdentimes.com/story/news/2003/03/24/us-soldiers-captured/32346206007/.*

[458] *Defeat Colonial Occupation of Iraq, THE INTERNATIONALIST, (June 2003) https://www.internationalist.org/defeatiraqoccupation.html.*

[459] *Id.*

attacks by "the enemy": "I have to give the guy credit. He has figured out how to stop us."[460]

Iraqi armed men and women in the southern city of Nasriya ambushed a supply column, that killed ten, wounded many more, and left an unknown number of U.S. soldiers unaccounted for.[461] Iraqi mortars, artillery cannons, rockets, and rifles destroyed U.S. army trucks and Humvees. Iraqi state TV broadcasted 5 captured US soldiers that next day while the Pentagon was enraged as matters only grew worse for them with the numbers of troops and mercenaries detained by the Iraqi Ground Forces.[462] The Iraqi Resistance detained countless invaders who crossed into Iraq illegally. 18 British soldiers died in the obliteration of a helicopter and US led battles

---

[460] *Defeat Colonial Occupation of Iraq, THE INTERNATIONALIST, (June 2003) https://www.internationalist.org/defeatiraqoccupation. html.*

[461] *Supra note 333, Woodward.*

[462] *Iraq Broadcasts Images of Five U.S. Prisoners of War, PBS (March 23, 2003) https://www.pbs.org/newshour/nation/ middle_east-jan-june03-prisoners_03-23.*

continued unsuccessfully in Umm Qasr.[463] Nor was Basra conquered: the British who originally intended to seize it remained stationed outside in fear.[464] Their fear was not without reason. It was in Basra later in 2007 when revolutionary combat intensified that the Mahdi Army took over a British military base and forced the colonial army to flee the city.[465] In 2003 the U.S. third infantry moved to the outskirts of Najaf where they failed to continue in the face of dedicated resistance. When a group of helicopters of the 101st airborne was called in, "the Iraqis threw up a wall of lead," said a U.S. analyst.[466] With only small arms fire, all 32 helicopters sustained

---

[463] *Troops face stiff resistance, THE CHRISTIAN SCIENCE MONITOR, (March 25, 2003) https://www.csmonitor.com/2003/0325/p25s03-woiq.html.*

[464] *Simon Akam, The Moment Britian's Army Knew It Was Lost, THE ATLANTIC, (Feb. 20, 2021) https://www.theatlantic.com/international/archive/2021/02/british-army-simon-akam/618015/.*

[465] *Aref Mohammed, British troops quit Iraqi city of Basra, REUTERS, (Sept. 3, 2007) https://www.reuters.com/article/idINIndia-29300820070903.*

[466] *Defeat Colonial Occupation of Iraq, THE INTERNATIONALIST, (June 2003) https://www.internationalist.org/defeatiraqoccupation.html.*

damages with two destroyed. The Iraqi guerilla warfare that followed and detained countless occupiers was even greater in intensity which US generals openly admit they lost to in their own words: "we were losing" – U.S. Navy Captain Raul A. Pete Pedrozo.[467] Iraqi testimonies state that the international imperialist press underreported the losses of the U.S. led coalition. When Iraqi revolutionaries obliterated three U.S. military trucks that took the lives of at least 18 troops in Diyala the controlled press only made brief mention of 3 soldiers killed quicky at the end of their segment.[468] [469] This was how the retreat and end of the U.S. occupation was portrayed if at all. Meanwhile the same media initiated a campaign to manipulate the world about events that developed across the region from Syria to Libya where numerous violations of the international rule of law occurred to our ignorance, or worst, tacit

---

[467] *COUNTERINSURGENCY LESSONS FROM IRAQ, 2009 WLNR 30846254*

[468] *See 9 U.S. soldiers killed in Iraq offensive, NBC NEWS, (Jan. 9, 2008) https://www.nbcnews.com/id/wbna22572707.*

[469] *Witnesses in Diyala*

consent.[470] The intended outcome of the censorship was to prevent the reversal of psychological defeat:

A.) Renewed impetus to the Palestinian cause and worldwide revolutionary struggle against imperialism empowered by the expulsion of thousands of troops through guerilla warfare in Iraq.

B.) US failures in Iraq undermine the authority, legitimacy, laws, prestige of US imperialism and proves to oppressed nations that victory remains achievable.

C.) Takeover of the US embassy and prosecution of US officials for war crimes illegally concealed by the media war funded by American imperialism.

D.) Diversion towards support for US backed regime change against non-compliant Arab states through the exploitation of the Arab Spring to advance colonial designs. All while the corporate media maintains complete silence on repression against Bahrain that witnessed the highest percentage of

---

[470] *Chomsky, N., & Herman, E. S. (1995). Manufacturing consent. Vintage.*

protestors in proportion to any other Arab state after 2011.[471]

Iraq, Syria, UN members, and solidarity movements who support their cause must work together to push for all available means towards the establishment of an International Tribunal of Iraq and Syria for the prosecution of major US violations comprised of deliberate misinformation campaigns that aided and abetted war crimes and genocide.

---

[471] *"Iran, Libya, and Syria are irresponsible regimes, which must be disarmed of weapons of mass devastation." – Ariel Sharon*

Rejection Of The Rule Of Law

The rights to the freedom of assembly, the freedom of religion, the freedom of expression, the right of **Habeas Corpus,** all faced increased repression since the "anti-terrorist" campaign of genocide against Iraq and greater Syria.[472] Attorney General John Ashcroft went so far as to condemn those who exercised their civil liberties as "aiding terrorists".[473] Even though Ashcroft and the US federal government waged wars to allegedly protect those very civil liberties. In the name of "liberty" US officials

---

[472] *Barron, J. A. (2002). Constitutional Law: Principles and Policy, Cases and Materials. United States: LexisNexis.*

[473] *At a Senate hearing in December 2001, U.S. Attorney General John Ashcroft openly attacked those who dared to complain about the assault on civil liberties: "Your tactics only aid terrorists for they erode our national unity and diminish our resolve. They give ammunition to America's enemies and pause to America's friends" (CNN.com, 7 December 2001).*

restricted habeas corpus and other rights to freedom while government surveillance expanded. Section 7 of the *Military Commission Act of 2006* permitted the unconstitutional suspension of the right to habeas corpus and trials that involved so called terrorists. Habeas corpus protects the rights of individuals from arbitrary detention without just cause.[474] Countless Muslims and Arabs from Iraq, Syria, and the general region, including all those who share their struggle, suffer discriminatory indefinite detention without charges or trials across America. This repression fundamentally denies the rule of law and the protection of individual rights in direct contradiction to the principles of the **Magna Carta**. However, two landmark Supreme Court cases *Boumediene v. Bush* [475] and *Rasul v. Bush*[476] upheld the rights of prisoners in the affirmation of their right to Habeas Corpus. The legislation established to wage the so-called war on terror violated domestic and international laws. *Boumediene*

---

[474] *Tyler, Amanda L. "A Second Magna Carta: The English Habeas Corpus Act and the Statutory Origins of Habeas Privilege." Notre Dame L. Rev. 91 (2015): 1949.*

[475] *Boumediene v. Bush*, **533 U.S. 723 (2008)**

[476] *Rasul v. Bush*, **542 U.S. 466 (2004)**

specifically stated that the *Military Commissions Act 2006* was an unconstitutional suspension of the right to Habeas Corpus.[477] These cases once again demonstrate the potential for relief through the US legal system against US officials. The US legal system was designed to perfect an oppressive social order, however, which requires the establishment of Revolutionary Courts to gain full justice.

Pursuant to the "Uniting for Peace" resolution of the **General Assembly from November 1950 (resolution 377 (V)),** the General Assembly can act if the Security Council fails to act because of the dissatisfaction of a permanent member.[478] This will take place when an act of aggression occurs along with imminent danger. The General Assembly can assess the context with a perspective to advisory Members on actions to re-establish world peace and security. Accordingly, the UN members – majority vote through the General Assembly – may bypass the veto of the U.S. to pass a Security Council resolution and directly establish an international criminal Tribunal to hold the U.S. accountable for war crimes in Iraq and

---

[477] *US Const. Suspension Clause Art. I, Sec. 9, cl. 2*

[478] *G.A. Res. 377(V)A (Nov. 3, 1950).*

greater Syria. The ICJ issued an international irrevocable judgment against the U.S. to pay reparations to Nicaragua which set a precedent in favor of nations that oppose U.S. imperialism such as greater Syria and Iraq.[479] In the meantime the absence of enforcement for reparations justifies expropriation to take back what was stolen.

Since 2016, the regime of the U.S. has worked toward the goal to dismantle entirely several international organizations committed to justice and to instead bolster criminal organizations with the greatest number of human right violations in the world. The International Criminal Court, which serves as a worldwide tribunal that investigates and prosecutes war crimes, acts of torture, and genocide, has the objective of this initiative dedicated to justice.

An American president issued an executive order that effectively made it a crime for anyone to work for

---

[479] *Military and Paramilitary Activities in and Against Nicaragua (Nicar. v. U.S.), Judgment, 1986 I.C.J. Rep. 14, ¶ 268 (June 27) [hereinafter Military and Paramilitary Activities in and Against Nicaragua]; see also Ryan Goodman & Michael Schmitt, Having Crossed the Rubicon: Arming and Training Syrian Rebels, JUST SEC. (Sept. 26, 2014), https://www.justsecurity.org/15660/crossed-rubicon-arming-training-syrian-rebels/.*

the ICC in response to the irrational American assertion that the investigation of the ICC into accusations of war crimes by the US in Syria and Iraq endangers national security.[480] This was done in a draconian response to the presidential claim that the investigation conducted by the ICC constitutes a threat to national security.[481] The United States normalized the cancellation of visas for attorneys, judges, human rights researchers, and workers, as well as freeze the finances of such individuals, and they may even ban them from entrance to the nation.[482]

Mike Pompeo, the Secretary of State, announced restrictions against Fatou Bensouda, the special prosecutor for the International Criminal Court, and her senior assistant.[483] This made it possible for U.S. citizens to face punishment if they "materially support" the International Criminal Court by activities such as submission of an

---

[480] *Exec. Order No. 13928, 3 C.F.R. § 36139 (June 11, 2020).*

[481] *Exec. Order No. 13928, 3 C.F.R. § 36139 (June 11, 2020).*

[482] *Id.*

[483] *Arwa Mahdawi, US imposes sanctions on top international criminal court officials, The Gaurdian, (Sept. 2, 2020) https://www.theguardian.com/law/2020/sep/02/us-sanctions-international-criminal-court-fatou-bensouda*

Amicus brief in favor of a case. The typical targets include human rights attorneys.[484] Biden maintained the restrictions on the ICC that concerns review of genocidal policies in Muslim and Arab nations which indicates that his half reversal was not driven by concern for human rights but to apply pressure on Russia for crimes America committed on a far greater scale with no oversight.

The US seeks to design colonial legislative bodies where it acts as both the prosecutor and the judge. Unfortunately, the United Nations has failed to achieve our aspirations with many bright promises. The principal problem for the UN was never due to the validity of principles and objectives accepted universally but rather with the means to translate these principles into reality. The fight in the UN and international courts for Iraq and Syria will utilize human rights law as a tool in the struggle to make the entirety of the international community conform to universally recognized legal principles they proclaim. Historically the recommendations of the General Assembly carried some weight that influenced policies of states to bring attention of world opinion on

---

[484] *Id.*

major global problems of **colonialism**. The debates in the assembly on such questions accelerated **decolonial processes and contributed to some degree towards the emancipation of many nations across the Global South.**

In April of 2017, the U.S. invaded Syria under the guise of liberation from a government legally recognized internationally and supported by the significant segments of the Syrian population.[485] Syrian representatives to the UN rightly spoke against this invasion.[486] Specifically, Dr. Bashar Jaafari said, "the Syrian Government calls on the UN Secretary-General to shoulder his responsibilities for preventing any aggression on Syria."[487] He stated that the U.S. government has repeated the same mistake the

---

[485] *A timeline of the US involvement in Syria's conflict, THE ASSOCIATED PRESS, (Jan. 11, 2019) https://apnews.com/ article/donald-trump-syria-islamic-state-group-middle-east-international-news- 96701a254c5a448cb253f14ab697419b.*

[486] *Syria asks UN to stop 'any aggression', THE CHRONICLE (Sept. 3, 2013) https://www.chronicle.co.zw/ syria-asks-un-to- stop-any-aggression/.*

[487] *Id.*

previous administrations made when the U.S. invaded Vietnam and in the Cuban crisis.[488] In an interview, Dr.

Bashar Jaafari questioned the results of the intended U.S. invasion of Syria, making it clear that the results will entail the death of Syrian women, children, and innocent civilians and lead, ultimately, to human rights abuses.[489] He stated that the US supported mercenaries in Syria against a legitimate government in a sovereign country.[490] **The Security Council Resolution 2139** establishes Syrian sovereignty, independence, unity, and territorial integrity[491]. It also calls on all actors to immediately cease all violence that has caused the Syrian people to suffer.

---

[488] *See Tim Anderson, Dr. Bashar Al-Jaafari: Why they 'punish' Syria, AL MAYADEEN ENGLISH, (Sept. 27, 2022) https://english.almayadeen.net/articles/feature/dr-bashar-al-jaafari:-why-they-punish-syria.*

[489] *U.S. Peace Council's Exclusive Interview with Dr. Bashar Ja'afari, Permanent Representative of the Syrian Arab Republic to the United Nations, and Head of the Syrian Delegation at the Geneva III Negotiations, U.S. PEACE COUNCIL, (Feb. 19, 2016) https://uspeacecouncil.org/u-s-peace-councils-exclusive-interview-with-dr-bashar-jaafari-permanent- representative-of-the-syrian-arab-republic-to-the-united-nations-andhead-of-the-syrian-delegation-at-the-g/.*

[490] *Id.*

[491] *S.C. Res. 2139 (2014).*

Even after Resolution 2118 the U.S. alliance continued to undertake military activities in Syria in violation of the Security Council Resolution.[492]

After the **Security Council Resolution 2401** was adopted by the Security Council a significant level of violence was escalated by US across the nation[493]. Diplomatic missions faced assaults in addition to innocent people, minorities, members of the majority, and health care centers, which further compounded the suffering and displacement of large numbers of people. This demands the legal responsibilities of all sides under international humanitarian law and international human rights law, in addition to relevant decisions of the Security Council, to end all aggression against Syrian sovereignty. The Syrian Arab Republic never invited America and proxies to invade or to participate in the coalition against ISIS which emerged out of U.S. Operation Timber Sycamore, the invasion of Iraq, and U.S. ties with the Gulf monarchies. The Republic of Iraq never invited the U.S. led coalition to launch the criminal war of aggression in 2003 that

---

[492] *S.C. Res. 2118 (2013).*

[493] *S.C. Res. 2401 (2018).*

significantly deteriorated the literacy rate and education system that once expanded exponentially at the highest rate in Iraqi history after the July 14 Revolution.[494] With regards to chemical weapons allegations: the US openly used white phosphorous against civilians in Raqqa and further evidence suggests that NATO backed groups employed nerve agents[495] unlike Syrian inspectors who welcomed experts to assess the presence of biological weapons. On my personal visit to Eastern Ghouta, the alleged site of Syrian government chemical attacks, the residents told me it was the Syrian army that protected them from the FSA rebels. An MIT report conducted with a former UN weapons inspector refuted US allegations against the Syrian government which adds to the credibility of the testimony I witnessed amid intense

---

[494] *Shakir Muhammad Usman & Mustafa Hamzah Mustafa, Iraq's Educational System: History and Rebuilding Process Post- Daesh, MANARA MAGAZINE, (July 2, 2022) https://manaramagazine. org/2022/07/iraqs-educational-system-history-and- rebuilding-process-post-daesh/.*

[495] *HRW concerned about phosphorus use by U.S. coalition in Raqqa, REUTERS, (June 14, 2017) https://www.reuters.com/article/ us-mideast-crisis-syria-phosphorous/hrw-concerned-about-phosphorus-use-by-u-s-coalition- in-raqqa-idUSKBN1951CY.*

conflict.[496] More evidence exists to suggest that the US military used chemical munitions in the mass slaughter of Arabs after Iraqi troops left Kuwait which extracted oil from the devastated Iraqi economy, yet Iraq continues to pay over 50 billion $ worth of reparations. Whereas the US has not returned any compensation for crimes of a far greater scale. The US military has carried out chemical attacks against civilian areas across Iraq and Syria for decades alongside its Israeli associates in crimes against Gaza.

Figure 8: Zionist attack against civilian transportation station in Syria

---

[496] *Richard Lloyd, Possible Implications of Faulty US Technical Intelligence in the Damascus Nerve Agent Attack of 8/21/13.*

The former Syrian permanent representative to the United Nations, Dr. Bashar al-Jaafari, asked the United Nations Security Council to take action to end the repeated Israeli transgressions against Syrian territories.[497] He inquired if it necessitated Syria to assert the right to self-defense and respond to the Israeli aggression on Damascus International Airport.[498] Al-Jaafari maintained that the Israeli aggressions against Syria was only made possible by the unrestricted assistance given to this criminal Zionist enterprise by the states that make up the permanent members of the UN. The applies in Iraq. The Syrian right to self-defense to reclaim the occupied Syrian Golan Heights remains unaffected by the continued American positions that inhibits the Security Council. The reintegration of the Golan Heights into the Syrian Arab Republic constitutes a fundamental right of the Syrian people not open to negotiations or compromise.

---

[497] *Al-Jaafari: Return of Golan to Syria sovereignty is firm, non-negotiable right, PERMANENT MISSION OF THE SYRIAN ARAB REPUBLIC TO THE UNITED NATIONS, (Jan. 22, 2019) https://www.un.int/syria/statements_speeches/al-jaafari-return-golan-syria-sovereignty-firm-non-negotiable-right.*

[498] *Id.*

The expulsion of Zionists from the Syrian Golan Heights requires application based on the principles of justice and international law and resolutions such as **No. 242[499], 338[500], and 497[501] from the Security Council.**

The efforts of the Zionist entity to change the situation in the Golan Heights with the recent annexation will not alter Syrian legal or sovereign rights over the territory they occupy. Neither will the illegitimate American presence in northeastern Syria and NATO in the form of the Turkish occupation of northern Syria. Zionists construct illegal settlements in The Golan Heights as a barrier from the rest of Syria. Zionists continue this policy of settlement expansion into lands rich with Syrian natural resources in complete disregard for international law and in obstruction of peaceful resolutions.[502] The consideration of the primary issues such as the continuation of settlement

---

[499] *S.C. Res. 242 (1967).*

[500] *S.C. Res. 338 (1973).*

[501] *S.C. Res. 497 (1981).*

[502] *Israel is changing the demographics of Golan Heights too, TRT WORLD, (June 1, 2021) https://www.trtworld.com/magazine/israel-is-changing-the-demographics-of-golan-heights-too-47171.*

establishment as "non- negotiable" renders void the very negotiations Zionist officials proclaim as the only way to solve the crisis. We can no longer ignore the daily atrocities and repressive tactics that the Israeli occupation commits against the people of the occupied Syrian Golan as their fighter jets strike the country on a regular basis. The Israeli intruders for years tried to impose segregationist education systems to separate the Druze population from their Syrian Arab roots as well as issue I.D. cards that clarified this distinction.[503] The unequivocal rejection of this effort by the Syrian masses of the Golan Heights who assert their Syrian Arab identity marks a failure for Israeli colonial ambitions and a victory for Syrian national unity against imperialism and Zionism. Given the sparsity of news from the occupied Golan Heights, the world remains unaware of the worldwide example of committed defiance and struggle to protest Zionist annexation with mass confrontations and a legitimately declared strike by residents of an occupied territory. The

---

[503] *See Jonathan Cook, The Druze have to face that in Israel, some are far more equal than others, MIDDLE EAST EYE, (Aug. 22, 2018) https://www.middleeasteye.net/opinion/ druze-have-face-israel-some-are-far-more-equal-others.*

unconditional release of political prisoner Sidqi al-Maqt in early 2020 marked a great achievement for Syria by his persistent struggle.[504] Sidqi al-Maqt struggled for liberation of the Golan Heights for years and was imprisoned by Israeli forces most recently due to his active exposure of collaboration between Israeli occupation forces and sectarian opposition factions.[505]

Bashar Al-Jaafari reaffirmed the Syrian claim to the Golan Heights and the commitment to support the right of the Palestinians to decide their own destiny and liberate all of Palestine as an independent state with Jerusalem as their capital.[506] In addition to the guaranteed right of refugees to return to their homes in accordance with

---

[504] *Israel to release man convicted of spying for Syria in swap deal, ALJAZEERA, (Jan. 10, 2020) https://www.aljazeera.com/ news/2020/1/10/israel-to-release-man-convicted-of-spying-for-syria-in-swap-deal.*

[505] *Israel to release man convicted of spying for Syria in swap deal, ALJAZEERA, (Jan. 10, 2020) https://www.aljazeera.com/ news/2020/1/10/israel-to-release-man-convicted-of-spying-for-syria-in-swap-deal.*

[506] *Al-Jaafari: restoration of occupied Syrian Golan will remain a priority for Syria, PERMANENT MISSION OF THE SYRIAN ARAB REPUBLIC TO THE UNITED NATIONS, (Oct. 28, 2019) https://www.un.int/syria/statements_speeches/al-jaafari-restoration- occupied-syrian-golan-will-remain-priority-syria.*

resolution No. 194 for 1948.[507] He appealed to the states complicit in the Zionist invasion to reevaluate their policies and positions and strive toward the restoration of rights to the people who previously held them.[508] The Iraqi Resistance established a Golan Liberation Brigade that has prepared to take actions to fully liberate the Golan Heights at the request of the Syrian government.[509] This defiance emerged after Texan congressmen took initiative to recognize the usurpation of the Syrian Golan Heights as legitimate while at the same time placed blockades on the Iraqi Revolutionary Army.[510]

---

[507] *G.A. Res. 194 (III), (Sept. 25, 1964).*

[508] *Supra note 331, Al-Jaafari: restoration of occupied Syrian Golan will remain a priority for Syria.*

[509] *Iraq Resistance Movement Establishes Brigade to Liberate Golan Heights, TASNIM NEWS AGENCY, (March 8, 2017) https://www. tasnimnews.com/en/news/2017/03/08/1349676/iraqi-resistance-movement-establishes-brigade-to-liberate- golan-heights.*

[510] *Sen. Cruz, Rep. Gallagher Introduce Bill to Lock in US Recognition of Israeli Sovereignty Over the Golan Heights, TED CRUZ: U.S. SENATOR FOR TEXAS, (May 14, 2021) https://www.cruz.senate. gov/newsroom/press-releases/sen-cruz-rep- gallagher-introduce-bill-to-lock-in-us-recognition-of-israeli-sovereignty-over-the-golan-heights.*

In his statement on the annual high-level debate held by the UN General Assembly, Faisal Mekdad claimed that hegemonic countries disregarded international law to impose "straightjacketed agendas," invest in extremism, and "place economies in a stranglehold."[511] U.S. imperialists use the pretext of freedom and human rights to justify their actions, but in the meantime, they commit crimes against humanity and destroy independent nations free of hegemony. In addition, he stated that the mercenaries who receive support from some nations cannot classify as "moderate".[512] In contrast, these extremist mercenaries work as tools employed to harm the countries that Western powers failed to conquer.

Certain hegemonic nations advocated "smart sanctions" when these actions constitute a kind of collective punishment and mass murder against revolutionary societies.[513] He argued that the war on

---

[511] *'The war on Syria has failed,' Foreign Minister says in UN speech, denouncing the West's hegemonic ambitions, UNITED NATIONS: NEWS, (Sept. 26, 2022) https://news.un.org/en/story/2022/09/1128011.*

[512] *Id.*

[513] *Id.*

Iraq and Syria belongs to a long history of unlawful activity and an attempt by the West to preserve global control.[514] However, efforts to isolate Syria internationally and defeat the will of the nation failed. Faisal Mekdad argued that the last decade greatly challenged the Syrian people, who endured incalculable losses from violence backed by the U.S. regime, assaults on the financial system, and the infliction of unilateral coercive power applied with ruthlessness.[515] Any illicit military presence in Syria violates Syrian sovereignty, and the fight against "terrorism" needs to take place with the approval of the Syrian Government in accordance with international law. Faisal Mekdad stressed that separatist opposition should refrain from assistance to the occupiers. He said that because of imperialist economic measures and open theft of oil by the US military, Syria lost an estimated $107 billion in petroleum income, which devastated the economic situation and hurt the livelihood of the Syrian masses.[516]

---

[514] *Id.*

[515] *Id.*

[516] *Id.*

In addition, he claimed that Syria will continue to pursue compensation for lost income and all necessary actions to ameliorate the humanitarian situation on the ground.[517] Syria has supported discussion for amnesty of internal opposition offenses to promote national reconciliation and stability. President Bashar al-Assad has decreed the release of thousands of prisoners. Feisal Mekdad claimed further that despite the hope for peace in the region, Israeli tactics[518] moved the Arab homeland to heightened levels of destabilization, that includes an advancement of military maneuvers, an expansion in illegal settlements, the diaspora, and discrimination.

The United Nations General Assembly voted on November 10, 1975 to declare Zionism "a form of racism and racial discrimination".[519] While this promised some reassurance of international allegiance to the principles

---

[517] *'The war on Syria has failed,' Foreign Minister says in UN speech, denouncing the West's hegemonic ambitions, UNITED NATIONS: NEWS, (Sept. 26, 2022) https://news.un.org/en/story/2022/09/1128011.*

[518] *Syria Arab Republic: Syria will continue to support the Palestinian people and their established rights, 2022 WLNR 39814235*

[519] *G.A. Res. 3379 (Nov. 10, 1975).*

of the UN Charter - the so called "State of Israel" has yet to face any accountability for the violation of over 60 UN resolutions in Palestine and greater Syria.[520] Violence constitutes a monopoly of the US led western imperialism woven into the very fabric of capitalism without respect to law. US imperialism entails violence to an unprecedented scale in the kidnap of Africa to force Africans into labor without any pay to accumulate profits for colonialism, the vicious imperialist wars against the Global South, theft and occupation of the Western hemisphere which has now expanded into Palestine, the fascist coups against Iraq, Chile, Iran to name a few, the colonial hold onto Puerto Rico, and wars that continue to ravage and pillage the planet since the inception of American settler colonialism. Capitalism creates a violent system with the center concentrated in the violent relationship between the exploiter and exploited, relationship of oppression, and constant struggle for the accumulation of capital. Reactionary capitalist violence has a criminal nature that always

---

[520] *Which accounts for the most violations of all other members of the UN combined*

resorts to yet self-defense establishes itself on justice.[521] No empire in history has ever conceded power ever without a struggle in all its forms. Particularly without a revolutionary struggle.

When the Zionists bombed the UN headquarters in Lebanon repeatedly[522] it was none other than Hezbollah that forced the Zionists to abide by international law. Neither the UN, National Security Council, the ICJ, ICC, or any international resolutions forced the occupiers out of Lebanon or Iraq. It was the resistance and their state sponsors in Damascus and Tehran that forced the occupiers out of their homeland. The struggle for Iraq, Syria, Palestine, and the oppressed nations of the world continues with or without international organizations like the United Nations. The only way the rogue US regime will face accountability for war crimes like My Lai or Qana requires aggression met with resistance. Where the United Nations fails to take serious action our united

---

[521] *Frantz Fanon et al., The wretched of the Earth (2021).*

[522] *Human Rights Watch. Israel/Lebanon: Israel Responsible for Qana Attack Indiscriminate Bombing in Lebanon a War Crime. Jul7 29, 2006*

peoples need to act on our own organizational capacities as the nation of Afghanistan has demonstrated when it caused the Commander in Chief of the US military to burst in tears as his troops fled the Islamic emirate in failure.

Conclusion

The US federal government must abide by the legal standards it expects others to abide by. We call on the global community comprised of the signatories that claim to adhere to these many international laws, treaties, and declarations to indict and hold the United States federal government civilly and criminally accountable for the continuous conspiracies it has designed and executed against Syria and Iraq. The track record of American imperialism remains evident. The legally significant facts cited in war crimes, violations of territorial integrity, rejection of peaceful resolutions, political internment, forced displacement, and genocidal war in attempt to enforce illegal colonialism render the Defendants guilty who must cease and desist the commissions of these crimes.

Principle I (Nuremberg Trial) Any person who commits an act which constitutes a crime under international law is responsible therefor and liable to punishment.[523]

Principle II The fact that internal law does not impose a penalty for an act which constitutes a crime under international law does not relieve the offender from responsibility under international law.[524]

All U.S. officials, that conducted and conspired to engage in major wars against Syria and Iraq that killed millions with the use of weapons of mass destruction in the name of their removal, warrant indictment before trial for violations of the **U.S. Constitution**[525]**, the United Nations Declaration of Human Rights**[526]**, the**

---

[523] *82 U.N.T.S. 279.*

[524] *Id.*

[525] *U.S. Const. art. II, cl. 2.*

[526] *G.A. Res. 217(a) (III), U.N. Doc. A/810 at 71 (1948).*

Hague Conventions of 1907[527] and 1923, the Genocide Convention[528] and the Geneva Conventions of 1949[529]. U.S. officials thereupon warrant criminal convictions and removal from an illegitimate government that owes Syria and Iraq compensation which thereafter requires dissolution for these high crimes and misdemeanors with the inclusion but not limitation to:

- The elimination of all options for political rather than military resolutions in the wars of aggression on Syria and Iraq without congressional approval in violation of the **United Nations Charter, the Nuremberg Charter, U.S. Constitution, among all the cited international and federal laws**

We respectfully request from the international community to declare judgement on our juridical claim.

---

[527] *Convention (No. IV) Respecting the Laws and Customs of War on Land 1907, 2 AJIL Supp. (1908).*

[528] *78 U.N.T.S. 277.*

[529] *75 U.N.T.S. 135; 75 U.N.T.S. 287.*

1. RECOGNITION OF THE SOVERIEGN RIGHT OF THE IRAQI AND SYRIAN PEOPLE

A.) The sacred struggle of the Arab, Kurdish, Assyrian, and Turkmen people in the land between the two rivers transcends Sykes Picot and belongs to the holy monotheistic religion of God as the property of all Muslims

B.) Recognition of the Iraqi & Syrian sovereign rights in solidarity with all oppressed nations committed to uproot imperialism through pan-Islamic, pan-Arab national liberation and international proletarian revolution

2. THE DEMAND FOR THE US FEDERAL GOVERNMENT TO RELINQUISH RULE

A.) The people of Iraq and Syria shall determine their own internal affairs without interference

B.) Evacuate all US troops, advisors, military personnel, contractors, and intelligence

C.) Dismantle all US military bases across the Muslim Society to which Iraq and Syria belong

D.) Cease US Baghdad Embassy Operations to replace with Embassy for Native Nations

E.) Respect the sovereignty, independence, unity, and territorial integrity of the Muslim Society

F.) The right to self-determination of the Muslim Society and release of all its political prisoners

G.) Emergency demand to lift the siege off Syria, Iran, and allied Iraqi Forces

H.) Reparations to all of Iraq, Syria, and the Muslim Society without condition

I.) Complete Liberation of the Golan Heights, Shebaa Farms, and all Historic Palestine

J.) End the "War on Terror", the Israeli occupation, and all forms of US military intervention

K.) Prosecution of US officials in the court systems of Syria, Islamic Republic, or the ICJ

L.) Promote the welfare of the Muslim Society to which Iraq and Syria belong

M.) Respect Native Sovereignty and the right to secession for internal colonies of the US

N.) The preservation of the inalienable rights of the Iraqi and Syrian diaspora

O.) The dissolution of the US federal government as a legal and political entity

P.) The US military needs to pay for the clean up of toxic waste it has produced

The struggle against imperialism constitutes a worldwide struggle on many fronts that finds its expression in the struggle of the cradle of civilizations. The people in the lands of Iraq and Greater Syria, more than anyone else, deeply cherish peace after the endurance of a war of aggression waged for years by the US government. Peace in dignity and honor. Never peace in slavery and humiliation. For over 50 years we endured all sacrifices and hardships, resolved to fight back aggression armed with centuries of experiences that date back to the triumph against the crusades since nothing has more value than independence and freedom.

The fact that US imperialism failed in Iraq and Syria in no way means its inevitable overthrow will come easy. In the wake of failures emerges unprecedented governmental crises. Crisis after crisis as statesmen search for a consolidation strategy while the rich grow richer at the expense of increased poverty that faces prison and efforts to sow divisions. The turmoil indicates fatal weakness in the system and offers great possibilities for revolutionary and popular movements. Revolution remains intimately tied to victories against imperialism worldwide. Those within the American imperialist state carry an urgent duty to liberate the earth from its toxic grip. Objective conditions will not produce revolution themselves. Such conditions demand revolutionary organization to provide coherence and direction to lead the struggle for the seizure of true political power and expropriation of all that the oppressors refuse to compensate to the oppressed.

The League of the Righteous in the Land of Abraham (AS) fight on the side of the oppressed and exploited masses of the world and neither transgress against anyone nor occupy any lands. Who engage in self-defense against those who aggress against our homeland. The Iraqi & Syrian people undertake the revolutionary struggle for national independence, peace, justice, and social progress of the peoples of the world. We reaffirm our unshakable determination to liberate all Greater Syria with the conviction that our just struggle will undoubtedly triumph. We will not compromise the freedom of Palestine.

Iraq & Syria will never belong to the elites of the USA or any monopoly capitalists. Iraq & Syria belongs to all Muslims and the native Arab, Turkmen, Assyrian, and Kurdish people. This we will defend and fight for until victory or martyrdom. The Iraqi & Syrian struggle for independence and liberation belongs to the revolution of the oppressed and exploited masses of the greater Arab and Islamic nation against oligarchies, capitalism, and imperialism. It also belongs to the international working-class revolution for a healthy sustainable alternative to capitalism. We will remain steadfast in the struggle to improve the condition of our oppressed nation and liberate the entirety of our homeland from the chains of occupation imposed by the enemies of peace. Through unity we build power and strength and will restore our inalienable rights.

The steadfast nation of Syria and Iraq refuses to submit to the tyranny of the USA super rich corporate ruling class. Our revolutionary forces will not sit idle and watch as the tyrants drain our lives before our very eyes. Instead, we will struggle until the overthrow of corrupted systems. Through our demands we seek relief for impoverished oppressed people. Through a unified struggle the deprived will find the power to win. Those greedy imperialists remain void of any human compassion and prey especially hard on the dispossessed. We call for all people to put pressure on these predators and their illusory ideology. These butchers will face justice as their greedy cutthroat world continues to crumble. They cannot stop the rage and determination of oppressed people.

Together we will end this nightmare death order they impose on us. We will fight for our salvation no matter the odds. Power to the courageous forces of liberation across this world. The power of the people remains greater than the technology of the wicked. The righteous battle the enemy with high combat spirit that gains strength by every new sacrifice without any fear of any supposed military might. The noble sons of Mesopotamia once again proved that the spirit of selflessness, sacrifice, steadfastness continues to flow in the veins of our beloved people in the land.

The enemies of peace failed to steam the fury of the oppressed and halt the demand for peace, justice, and dignity. We will never simply rely on the courts of imperialism alone for relief. They belong to the very system that we combat actively. Our determination and our faith lie with the oppressed & exploited of the world who stopped the invasions of Lebanon and Iraq without the help of the UN. None of the imperialists who still seem outwardly strong will avoid the doom ordained by history. If protests fail to hasten their ultimate defeat, then we will use whatever exists in the constitution to preserve this world and future generations. The people of America and the people of Iraq & Syria share a common enemy whom we will not allow make us enemies.

The constitution was written by architects of genocide and forced labor as codified in the 13th amendment. The struggle continues even when it will require us to work outside the framework of government-controlled opposition that only exists to foster an illusion of democracy. We will not operate under any delusion that freedom will come from the American constitution but only use it as a tool when necessary to advance the interests of the oppressed. Each attack by American warplanes cost the annual salary of a teacher in the US while an entire week of attacks amounts to millions of dollars that will open schools across entire states. The fuel burned in one hour by a jet costs the same price for food to feed a family of four over the span of two and a half months but instead it only produces hazardous waste. The struggle for Iraq and Syria serves as a symbol of the collective fight against oppression that we possess the right to resist and organize against.

Based on the aforementioned: we emphasize the significance to continue the struggle to regain the rights and dignity of our nation. The morale & number of revolutionaries increase daily day while on the contrary the colonial forces suffer the lowest level of recruitment levels in history. We will not tire or relent until we drive you out of West Asia. Power through unity to alleviate our conditions, rehabilitate our homeland, and heal our pain & wounds with a peaceful, prosperous, and sovereign life under the shade of justice in a liberated Palestine.

We will never tolerate the dishonorable occupation of neither Iraq nor Syria. The enemy has retreated on the run from Afghanistan and most of Iraq in fear of a resistance movement they cannot see nor predict. We will strive against them until they leave the remainder of our land submissively. The brave Iraqi Insurgency remains a thorn in the hearts of their enemies. The noble sons of Iraq prove that the spirit of sacrifice, sincerity, and steadfastness continues to flow in the veins our beloved people in our blessed land. The invasion will face the same fate in Syria as Iraq and Afghanistan by the will of God.

In memory of Shahid Salih Kaso martyred in the struggle against Zionism & imperialism who proved the reality of the war on Syria that took the lives of 40 relatives to date in 2022

Syrian Arab Army parades one of hundreds of destroyed Israeli tanks that invaded Lebanon

Shahid Salih Kaso destroyed seven Merkava tanks of the Zionist invaders in 1982 when Hezbollah emerged

Index

November 30, 2022, from https://nsarchive.gwu.
edu/briefing-book/cuba-intelligence/2020-10-   09/
che- guevara-cia-mountains-bolivia

H. (2021, July 25). *1954 Convention for the Protection
of Cultural Property in the Event of Armed
Conflict*. UNESCO. Retrieved November 30, 2022,
from   https://n.unesco.org/protecting-   heritage/
convention-and-protocols/1954-convention

Kadri, Ali. *The Unmaking of Arab Socialism*. Anthem
Press, 2016. https://doi.org/10.2307/j.ctt1hj9zdb

Falk, Richard A. The Costs of War: International Law,
the UN, and World Order After Iraq. United Kingdom,
Routledge, 2008.

General Assembly, U. N. (n.d.). *A/RES/30/3452 - Declaration on the Protection of All Persons from Being Subjected to Torture and Other Cruel, Inhuman or Degrading Treatment or Punishment - UN Documents: Gathering a body of global agreements.* A/RES/30/3452 - Declaration on the Protection of All Persons From Being Subjected to Torture and Other Cruel, Inhuman or Degrading Treatment or Punishment - UN Documents: Gathering a Body of Global Agreements. Retrieved November 30, 2022, from http://www.un- documents.net/a30r3452.htm

Abdul Aziz al Khair. (n.d.). The World From PRX. Retrieved November 30, 2022, from https://theworld. org/person/abdul-aziz-al-khair

Chapter I: Article 2(30)–(5) — Charter of the United Nations — Repertory of Practice of United Nations Organs — Codification Division Publications. (2021, March 10). Chapter I: Article 2(1)–(5) — Charter of the United Nations — Repertory of Practice of United Nations Organs — Codification Division Publications. Retrieved November 30, 2022, from https://legal.un.org/repertory/ art2.shtml

Torture, American Style. Publication #3 of Historians Against the War (HAW). Publisher: Historians Against the War. Volume Number: No. 3. Format: Periodical Collection: Prison – Statistics

From Attica to Abu Ghraib (April – May, 2005). Reflections by Political Prisoners in the U.S., Sundiata Acoli. Publisher: Jericho Amnesty Movement (1995). Volume Number: April-May Format: Monograph Collection: Political Prisoners- General Info

'The war on Syria has failed,' Foreign Minister says in UN speech, denouncing the West's hegemonic ambitions. (2022, September 26). UN News. Retrieved November 30, 2022, from https://news.un.org/en/story/2022/09/1128011

International Tribunal of Indigenous Peoples and Oppressed Nations in the USA and _the Verdict of the Special International Tribunal on the Violation of Human Rights of Political Prisoners and Prisoners of Wars in United States Prisons and Jails._

Al-Jaafari: Return of Golan to Syria sovereignty is firm, non-negotiable right | Syria. (2019, January 22). Al-Jaafari: Return of Golan to Syria Sovereignty Is Firm,

Non-negotiable Right | Syria. Retrieved November 30, 2022, from https://www.un.int/syria/statements speeches/al- jaafari-return-golan-syria- sovereignty-firm-non-negotiable-right

Over 70 ICC Nations Support Court and Oppose US Sanctions. (2020, November 3). NECN. Retrieved November 30, 2022, from https://www.necn.com/news/national-international/over-70- icc-nations- support-court-and-oppose-us-sanctions/2342667/

UN General Assembly Resolution 377-C (November 1950). (n.d.). UN General Assembly Resolution 377- C (November 1950). Retrieved November 30, 2022, from https://www.jewishvirtuallibrary.org/un- general-assembly-resolution-377-c-november-1950

Tokyo War Crimes Trial | The National WWII Museum | New Orleans. (n.d.). The National WWII Museum | New Orleans. Retrieved November 30, 2022, from https://www.nationalww2museum.org/war/topics/tokyo-war-crimes-trial

UN tribunal convicts 3 Rwandan media executives for their role in 1994 genocide. (2003, December 3). UN News.

Retrieved November 30, 2022, from https://news.un.org/en/story/2003/12/87282

International War Crimes Tribunal Records TAM.098. (n.d.). International War Crimes Tribunal Records TAM.098. Retrieved November 30, 2022, from http://dlib.nyu.edu/findingaids/html/tamwag/tam_098/bioghist.html

The U.S. does not recognize the jurisdiction of the International Criminal Court. (2022, April 16). NPR.org. Retrieved November 30, 2022, from https://www.npr.org/2022/04/16/1093212495/the-u-s- does-not-recognize-the-jurisdiction-of-the- international-criminal-court

Adnan Pachachi. *Iraq's Voice at the United Nations 1959-69.* Quarter Books Limited 1991

Clark, Ramsey. *War Crimes: A Report on United States War Crimes Against Iraq.* United States, Maisonneuve Press, 1992.

Nasrallah, Hassan. *The Voice of Hezbollah: Transcripts of the General Secretary's Speeches*

Legal Disputes Under Article 36(2) of the Statute (From International Court of Justice at a Crossroads, P 183-222, 1987, Lori Fisler Damrosch, ed. -- See NCJ-122854) | Office of Justice Programs. (1987, January 1). Legal Disputes Under Article 36(2) of the Statute (From International Court of Justice at a Crossroads, P 183-222, 1987, Lori Fisler Damrosch, Ed. -- See NCJ-122854) | Office of Justice Programs. Retrieved November 30, 2022, from https://www.ojp.gov/ncjrs/virtual-library/abstracts/legal-disputes- under-article-362-statute- international-court

The Case Against the Death Penalty. (n.d.). American Civil Liberties Union. Retrieved November 30, 2022, from https://www.aclu.org/other/case-against-death-penalty

America at a Crossroads. The Trial of Saddam Hussein | PBS. (n.d.). America at a Crossroads. The Trial of Saddam Hussein | PBS. Retrieved November 30, 2022, from https://www.pbs.org/weta/crossroads/about/show_trial.html

Taguba Report: AR 15-6 Investigation of the 800th Military Police Brigade - Certified Copy. (209 C.E., January 1). www.thetorturedatabase.org. Retrieved November

30, 2022, from https://www.thetorturedatabase.org/
document/ar-15-6-investigation-800th-military-police-
investigating- officer-mg-antonio-taguba-taguba-

U.S. Treatment of Prisoners in Iraq: Selected Legal Issues.
(2005, October 27). U.S. Treatment of Prisoners in Iraq:
Selected Legal Issues - EveryCRSReport.com. Retrieved
November 30, 2022, from https://www.everycrsreport.
com/reports/RL32395.html

Wilson, J. (2005, November 16). *US admits using
white phosphorus in Falluja.* The Guardian. Retrieved
November 30, 2022, from http://www.theguardian.com/
world/2005/nov/16/iraq.usa

Claudia Wright, "Generals' Assembly: The Secrets of
US Turkish Military Planning," New Statesmen (15
July 1983): 20. PO 371 / 133791 Sir John Baker. British
Embassy in Ankara 1106. July 16 (Secret and Urgent) 72
Baghdad 2758, March 26, 1959, *Op.Cit.,* p.398.

In Envisioning the Arab Future: Modernization in US-
Arab Relations, Nathan J. Citino US covert intervention

1958-1963 William Zeman National Security Action Memorandum No. 177, 7 August 1962, NSF, Robert W. Komer, box 413, Counterinsurgency, Police Program 1961–1963, Folder 3, JFKL; Rosenau, "The Kennedy Administration," 82–84, 97n128, 97n129.

Rattan, J. (2019). Changing Dimensions of Intervention Under International Law: A Critical Analysis. *SAGE Open, 9*(2), 2158244019840911.

Hage Ali, M. (2018). Hizbullah's Reconstruction of History. In *Nationalism, Transnationalism, and Political Islam* (pp. 93-132). Palgrave Macmillan, Cham.

Jalloh, C. C. (2020). The International Law Commission's First Draft Convention on Crimes Against Humanity: Codification, Progressive Development, or Both? *Case W. Res. J. Int'l L., 52*, 331.

Gillen, D., & Gonzalez, L. (2022). Donald Rumsfeld (1932–2021). *History in the Making, 15*(1), 14.

Arnold, P., & Sprumont, D. (2019). The "Nuremberg Code": Rules of public international law. In *Ethics Codes in Medicine* (pp. 84-96). Routledge.

Andemariam, S. W., & Berhe, I. T. (2020). The 2000 Algiers Agreement and the 2018 Asmara/Jeddah Peace Agreements Between Eritrea and Ethiopia: Continuity or a New Beginning? In *Ethiopian Yearbook of International Law 2019* (pp. 117-139). Springer, Cham.

Jean Luc, K. C. (2022). Principle of Sovereign Equality and Non-Interference in the Internal Affairs of A State. *Tirtayasa Journal of International Law, 1*(1), 59-75.

Mackin, A. (2022). *Violence, Sectarianism, and Decolonization: Re-Framing the Syrian Revolution* (Doctoral dissertation, University of Toronto (Canada)).

Rizvi, A. The Extrajudicial Killing of General Soleimani, and the Right to Life under International Law.

Weiler, Y. A., & Callamard, A. (2020). Qassem Soleimani: When the US distorts self-defense into assassination.

Bock, S., & Conze, E. (2021). United Nations General Assembly Resolution 3314 (XXIX) of 14 December 1974. *Rethinking the Crime of Aggression: International and Interdisciplinary Perspectives*, 291.

Hedlund, B. (2018). The right to life, A case research on how article 4 of the American Convention on Human Rights is connected to the act on forced disappearance, according to the Inter-American Court on Human Rights.

Deutschmann, D., & Garcia, M. D. C. A. (Eds.). (2022). *The Che Guevara Reader: Writings on Politics & Revolution*. Seven Stories Press.

Ikäheimo, E. SELF-DEFENSE AGAINST NON-STATE ACTORS IN AFGHANISTAN AND SYRIA.

Grant, K. A., & Kaussler, B. (2020). The battle of Aleppo: external patrons and the victimization of civilians in civil war. *Small Wars & Insurgencies, 31*(1), 1-33.

Eide, A. (2021). Militarisation with a Global Reach: A Challenge to Sovereignty, Security and the International

Legal Order. In *Problems of Contemporary Militarism* (pp. 299-322).

Routledge.

Nwogu, K., & Oraeto, A. C. (2021). Contextual Expansion Of The Right Of Self-Determination. Kilcullen, D. (2020). *The dragons and the snakes: How the rest learned to fight the west*. Oxford University press, USA.

Riedel, B. (2019). *Beirut 1958: How America's Wars in the Middle East Began*. Brookings Institution Press.

Koçak, H. (2020). Development of Self-Determination Right and The Role of Icj: Statements on The South West Africa (Namibia) Advisory Opinion. *Alınteri Sosyal Bilimler Dergisi, 4*(1), 47- 68.

Dörr, O., & Schmalenbach, K. (2018). *Vienna convention on the law of treaties*. Springer.

Assembly, U. G. (2022). *International Covenant on Economic, Social and Cultural Rights, International Covenant on Civil and Political Rights and Optional*

Protocol to the International Covenant on Civil and Political Rights, 16 December 1966. A/RES/2200.

Assembly, G. GA Res. 73/158, The Right of the Palestinian People to Self-Determination (Dec. 17, 2018).

Iverson, J. (2021). Contemporary Legal Content of Jus Post Bellum. In *Jus Post Bellum: The Rediscovery, Foundations, and Future of the Law of Transforming War into Peace* (pp. 232- 283). Brill Nijhoff.

Joarder, B. (2022). Comprehensive Prohibition of Torture: Challenges and Loosening of a Taboo. In *Human Rights and International Criminal Law* (pp. 164-192). Brill Nijhoff.

Arman, J., Henckaerts, J. M., Hiemstra, H., & Krotiuk, K. (2020). The updated ICRC Commentary on the Third Geneva Convention: A new tool to protect prisoners of war in the twenty-first century. *International Review of the Red Cross, 102*(913), 389-416.

Hartig, A. L. (2022). The Crime of Aggression: The Fall of the Supreme International Crime?. In *International*

Conflict and Security Law (pp. 1111-1137). TMC Asser Press, The Hague.

Trahan, J. (2022). Vetoes and the UN Charter: the obligation to act in accordance with the 'Purposes and Principles' of the United Nations. *Journal on the Use of Force and International Law*, 1-35.

Kirakosyan, M. (2022). Democratization in the Light of the Evolution of Chapter 7 Powers of the UN Charter: The Case of Iraq. *Democracy and Security*, 1-23.

Paige, T. P. (2019). Chemical Weapons (2013): Resolution 2118. In *Petulant and Contrary: Approaches by the Permanent Five Members of the UN Security Council to the Concept of threat to the peace' under Article 39 of the UN Charter* (pp. 216-223). Brill Nijhoff

Boys, J. D. (2018). The Clinton administration's development and implementation of cybersecurity strategy (1993–2001). *Intelligence and National Security*, *33*(5), 755-770.

Pfiffner, J. P. (2018). Decisionmaking, intelligence, and the Iraq war. In *Intelligence and national security policymaking on Iraq* (pp. 213-232). Manchester University Press.

Hartenian, L. (2021). *George W Bush Administration Propaganda for an Invasion of Iraq: The Absence of Evidence.* Routledge.

Kamal, M. H. M. (2019). Principles of Distinction, Proportionality and Precautions under the Geneva Conventions: the Perspective of Islamic Law. In *Revisiting the Geneva Conventions: 1949-2019* (pp. 244- 261). Brill Nijhoff.

Hobeika, M. (2022). *Reconstructing the neutrality and objectivity tenet in community interpretation: the case of Syrian refugees Lebanon* (Doctoral dissertation, Notre Dame University-Louaize).

Jazairy, I. (2019). Unilateral economic sanctions, international law, and human rights. *Ethics & International Affairs, 33*(3), 291-302.

Guerra, S. C. S., & da Silva, Á. S. F. (2021). Analysis of the incursion of international law of catastrophes to the normative territory of armed conflicts: when catastrophe and war collide. *Cadernos de Dereito Actual*, (16), 8-23.

Kadri, A. (2019). *Imperialism with reference to Syria*. Springer Singapore Sorensen, C. (2020). *Understanding the war industry*. SCB Distributors.

Yadon, L. J. (2018). *The Greatest Navy SEAL Stories Ever Told*. Rowman & Littlefield.

Hakki, L., Stover, E., & Haar, R. J. (2020). Breaking the silence: Advocacy and accountability for attacks on hospitals in armed conflict. *International Review of the Red Cross, 102*(915), 1201-1226.

Navruzov, A. A. (2019). A Cynical Enterprise: US-Iraq Relations, Oil, and the Struggle for the Persian Gulf.

Orford, A. (2021). *International Law and the Politics of History*. Cambridge University Press.

Hironobu, S. (2020). "As if" acting under Chapter VII of the UN Charter? Rigidity of the threshold between Chapter VII and non-Chapter VII. In *Asian Yearbook of International Law, Volume 13 (2007)* (pp. 103-125). Brill Nijhoff.

Byers, M. (2021). Still agreeing to disagree: international security and constructive ambiguity. *Journal on the use of force and international law, 8*(1), 91-114.

Rothe, D. L., & Medley, C. (2019). Beyond State and State-Corporate Crime Typologies: The Symbiotic Nature, Harm, and Victimization of Crimes of the Powerful and Their Continuation. *The Handbook of White-Collar Crime*, 81-94.

Alito, S., Anderson, J., Celebrezze, A. V., & Ansolabehere, S. Article II, Section 1, US Constitution, 30, 187, 194, 201–2 association, 39 collective action and, 35–6 exit, freedom of, and, 46–50.

Shiri, A., & Jafarpour Sadegh, E. (2021). Governing Requirements on the Criminalization of State Crimes in Iran's Criminal Policy Process. *Public Policy, 7*(4), 143-162.

Mitchell, J. (2020). *Poisoning the Pacific: The US Military's Secret Dumping of Plutonium, Chemical Weapons, and Agent Orange.* Rowman & Littlefield.

Chinnappa, A. E. (2019). The United States and the Coalition Provisional Authority—occupation by proxy?. *Leiden Journal of International Law, 32*(3), 415-436.

Blomdahl, M. (2019). Changing the conversation in Washington? An illustrative case study of President Trump's air strikes on Syria, 2017. *Diplomacy & Statecraft, 30*(3), 536-555.

Ramesh, R. (2019). *The History and Evolution of American Torture and Secret Prisons (1898- 2008)* (Doctoral dissertation).

Taguba, A. M. (2022). *US Army 15-6 report of abuse of prisoners in Iraq.* DigiCat.

Gaer, F. (2020). The Committee Against Torture: implementing the prohibition against torture. *Research Handbook on Torture*, 128-153.

Mbuayang, C. (2020). Balancing the Minimum Requirement to a Fair Trial in International Criminal Proceedings. *Available at SSRN 3525626.*

Roberts, M. J. (2020). The CIA War in Kurdistan: The Untold Story of the Northern Front in the Iraq War.

Caracciolo, I. (2021). UN Actions and Programs in Safeguarding the Independence of Judges. In *The Rule of Law in Europe* (pp. 111-135). Springer, Cham.

Toomey, L. (2019). The right to conscientious objection to military service: Recent jurisprudence of the United Nations working group on arbitrary detention. *Human Rights Law Review, 19*(4), 787-810.

Alamgir, M. Access to Justice: Concept, Development and State Responsibility to Promote It. *Judicial Administration Training Institute*, 139.

Tignino, M., & Bréthaut, C. (2020). The role of international case law in implementing the obligation not to cause significant harm. *International Environmental Agreements: Politics, Law and Economics, 20*(4), 631-648.

Lubowa, D. (2018). International Criminal Tribunal for Rwanda in the spotlight: analysing the limitations, shortcomings and legacy. *Africa Nazarene University Law Journal, 6*(2), 32-46.

Steelman, D. C. (2022). The Legal Legacy of the Special Court for Sierra Leone. In *IJCA* (Vol. 13, p. 1).

Burgis-Kasthala, M., & Saouli, A. (2022). The politics of normative intervention and the Special Tribunal for Lebanon. *Journal of Intervention and Statebuilding, 16*(1), 79-97.

Lilja, M., & Baaz, M. (2021). The unfortunate omission of entangled resistance in the 'local turn' in peace-building: the case of 'forced marriage' in the Extraordinary Chambers in the Courts of Cambodia (ECCC). *Conflict, Security & Development, 21*(3), 273-292.

Prakash, B. (2021). US Sanctions on International Criminal Court.

Al-hanhanah, A. N. M., & Fei, M. (2021). Upholding Human Rights and International Law in the Combat against International Terrorism. *JL Pol'y & Globalization*, *110*, 103.

Bdiwi, G. (2021). Ongoing crimes and the unlikelihood of punishment-Syria as a case study.

De la Rosa, M. V. M., & Romero, E. D. (2019). A modality-based approach to the United Nations Security Council's ambiguous positioning in the resolutions on the Syrian armed conflict. *Intercultural Pragmatics*, *16*(4), 363-387.

Kydd, A. H. (2022). Penalizing Atrocities. *International Organization*, 1-34.

Bracka, J. (2021). Legal Dimensions of the Conflict and Legacies of Human Rights Abuse. In *Transitional Justice for Israel/Palestine* (pp. 29-103). Springer, Cham.

Peou, S. (2019). Why smart sanctions still cause human insecurity. *Asian Journal of Peacebuilding, 7.*

Eilam, E. (2022). *Israel's National Security, the Arab Position, and Its Complicated Relations with the United States.* Rowman & Littlefield.

Grossman, J. (2022). Diaspora, Delegitimisation, and Foreign Policy: Unpacking Brazil's Vote for the "Zionism is Racism" United Nations Resolution. *Diplomacy & Statecraft, 33*(3), 518-542

Khanafer, Z. (2020). *The Lebanese Civil War: Effects on the Contemporary Political System* (Master's thesis, Eastern Mediterranean University (EMU)-Doğu Akdeniz Üniversitesi (DAÜ))

"A Short History of Neo-Colonialism" Vietnamese Studies. Nguyen Khag Vien Halla to Gleason, March 27, 1959, folder: CP Iraq [5], box 4, Special Staff File Series, White House Office: NSC Staff Papers, 1948- 1961, DDEL.

Palestine Liberation Army; We Will Return. Book found in Museum established by Iraqi Revolutionary Jawad al-Ta'i.

271

Baghdad, Mutanabi Street. Iraqi Ministry of Justice. Iraq Public Law 106 http://www.iraqld.iq/LoadLawBook. aspx?SC=081120057960790

Rare Glimpse Into Inner Workings Of American Empire In Middle East. "They revealed that basic U.S. policy was to maintain a U.S.-led system of regional order so that the U.S. government could influence how all parts of the world gained access to the region's oil." http://lobelog. com/rare- glimpse-into-inner- workings-of-american-empire-in-middle-east/Memorandum from Joint Chiefs of Staff to the Secretary of Defense, August 15, 1963, IRAQ 1961– 1963, box 426, Robert W. Komer, NSF, JFKL. "US arms policy in Iraq should be pursued with the ultimate objective … [the] open alignment of Iraq and Syria with the West."

Claudia Wright, "Generals' Assembly: *The Secrets of US-Turkish Military Planning*," New Statesmen (15 July 1983)

Dana Adams Schmidt, *"CIA Head Warns of Danger in Iraq,"* New York Times , 29 April 1959, A1.

Iraqi Ministry of Justice. Iraqi Legal Record http://www. iraqld.iq/LoadLawBook.aspx?SC=081120057960790

Document signed by Qasim. Ministry of Defense. Republic of Iraq. Al-Jannabi Qasim era archives. Baghdad

Al-Jannabi Qasim era archives. *Armed struggle Palestine Majalat al Dirasat Al Filasteeniya* Volume 9 issue 35 1998

Department of State. Division of Biographic Intelligence. *Al-Mahdawi, Fadhil 'Abbas (Col.) Memo.* Eisenhower Presidential Library, March 1959.

Memorandum from Bracken and Davies to Talbot, June 20, 1963, DEF 19, box 2, Records of the Country Director, RG 59, USNA; Bass, Support Any Friend, 111.

Samii, *"Role of SAVAK,"* 149-152; London A-2294 to State, March 8, 1967, RG59, CFPF 1967-1969, Box2218

Senate Select Committee to Study Governmental Operations with Respect to Intelligence Activities (Church Committee), *Interim Report: Alleged Assassination Plots Involving Foreign Leaders,* 94th Cong. 1st sess. (washington,

DC: Government Printing Office, 1975), 181 n1. Testimony by CIA personnel indicated that the colonel for whom the handkerchief was intended later "[s]uffered a terminal illness before a firing squad in Baghdad."

Sale, "Exclusive: Saddam Key in Early CIA Plot," *op. cit.*

Con Coughlin, *Saddam: King of Terror*, 3739; Aburish, *A Brutal Friendship*, 136137; John Bulloch and Harvey Morris, *Saddam's War: The Origins of the Kuwait Conflict and the International Response* (London, 1991), 5455.

Claudia Wright, "Generals' Assembly: The Secrets of US Turkish Military Planning," New Statesmen (15 July 1983): 20. PO 371 / 133791 Sir John Baker. British Embassy in Ankara 1106. July 16 (Secret and Urgent) Baghdad 2758, March 26, 1959, *Op.Cit.*, p.398.

FO 371/134198, From Washington to FO 14 July 1958

National Security Action Memorandum No. 177, 7 August 1962, NSF, Robert W. Komer, box 413, Counter insurgency, Police Program 1961–1963, Folder 3, JFKL; Rosenau, *"The Kennedy Administration,"* 82–84, 97n128,

97n129. The same Chicago police department that killed Fred Hampton trained anti-communist forces responsible for arguably the worst cold war massacre in history

IRAQ–IPS, NACP; F. Gulick, "IRAQ—Western-Trained Officials," 9 April 1963, RG 59, Lot File 66 D 470, box 1, AID 10, NACP

Limericks and Songs of War, Peace, and the Middle East. Producers: Lincoln Bergman. 9/29/1990. Speech against US war against Iraq that recalls anti-war mobilizations against military deployments to contain the July 14 Iraqi Revolution

Bundy to MacNamara, "National Security Action Memorandum No. 56," 28 June 1961, RG 286 (records of the United States Agency for International Development), USAID, Office of Public Safety, Office of the Director, box 5, IPS, National Security Council, National Archives College Park (hereafter NACP).

Riddleberger to Baghdad embassy, 11 February 1961, RG 286, Operations Division Africa Near East South

Asia, Subject File, box 62, IRAQ–IPS, NACP; F. Gulick, "IRAQ—Western-Trained Officials," 9 April 1963, RG 59, Lot File 66 D 470, box 1, AID 10, NACP

Al-Ahram, 27 September 1963. Cited in Batatu, Hanna. *The Old Social Classes and the Revolutionary Movements of Iraq: A Study of Iraq's Old Landed and Commercial Classes and of Its Communists, Ba'thists, and Free Officers.* London: Saqi, 2004.

Batatu, Hanna. *The Syria's Peasantry, the Descendants of its Lesser Rural Notables, and Their Politics Al-Hadaf* 1982. PFLP Documents English. pflpdocuments.org

Printed in the United States
by Baker & Taylor Publisher Services